Denmark and Norway 1940

Hitler's boldest operation

Campaign • 183

Denmark and Norway 1940

Hitler's boldest operation

Douglas C Dildy • Illustrated by John White

First published in Great Britain in 2007 by Osprey Publishing,
Midland House, West Way, Botley, Oxford OX2 0PH, UK
443 Park Avenue South, New York, NY 10016, USA
E-mail: info@ospreypublishing.com

A CIP catalogue record for this book is available from the British Library

ISBN: 978 1 84603 117 5

Page layout by: The Black Spot
Index by Alan Thatcher
Typeset in Helvetica Neue and ITC New Baskerville
Maps by The Map Studio Ltd
3D bird's-eye views by The Black Spot
Originated by United Graphics, Singapore
Printed in China through Worldprint Ltd.

07 08 09 10 11   10 9 8 7 6 5 4 3 2 1

For a catalogue of all books published by Osprey please contact:

NORTH AMERICA
Osprey Direct, c/o Random House Distribution Center, 400 Hahn Road,
Westminster, MD 21157
E-mail: info@ospreydirect.com

ALL OTHER REGIONS
Osprey Direct UK, P.O. Box 140 Wellingborough, Northants, NN8 2FA, UK
E-mail: info@ospreydirect.co.uk

www.ospreypublishing.com

FRONT COVER: Bundesarchiv Bild 101I-761-221-N-06

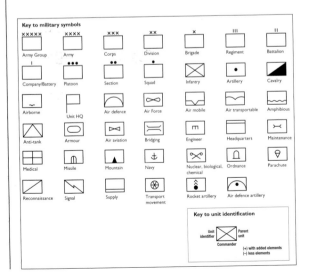

Author's note

The author would like to acknowledge his gratitude for the
generous support and assistance of several key individuals.
First to Mr Mark Horan, whose vast archive of primary
source materials on the RN and FAA in 1940 and detailed
knowledge were indispensable. Also to Mr John Dell
who provided much information on the Blackburn Skua,
its exploits and colouring. My thanks, too, go to noted
historian Dr Don Alberts for his critical review, corrections
and suggestions. Additionally I would like to acknowledge
the inspiration and encouragement of Professor Jim
Sanders of the US Navy Postgraduate School. Also to my
fellow enthusiasts of small nations' militaries: Arild Kjærås
of Norway, Kai Willadsen of Denmark and my friend John
Tate. Finally to the photographic experts who helped locate
and provide some notably rare photographs for this book:
Matthew Bailey of the National Portrait Gallery, Yvonne
Oliver of the Imperial War Museum and Brigitte Kuhl of the
German Bundesarchiv. To all these people I owe a huge
debt of thanks, but to none more so than to my wife, Ann,
who was a constant encourager and supporter throughout
the experience of compiling and writing the story of
history's first joint campaign, the German invasion of
Denmark and Norway in 1940.

Artist's note

Imperial War Museum Collections

Many of the photos in this book come from the Imperial
War Museum's huge collections which cover all aspects
of conflict involving Britain and the Commonwealth since
the start of the twentieth century. These rich resources
are available online to search, browse and buy at
www.iwmcollections.org.uk. In addition to Collections
Online, you can visit the Visitor Rooms where you can
explore over 8 million photographs, thousands of hours
of moving images, the largest sound archive of its kind
in the world, thousands of diaries and letters written by
people in wartime, and a huge reference library. To make
an appointment, call (020) 7416 5320, or e-mail
mail@iwm.org.uk. Imperial War Museum www.iwm.org.uk

CONTENTS

ORIGINS OF THE CAMPAIGN

The development of the situation in Scandinavia requires … The occupation of Denmark and Norway by a part of The German Armed Forces. This operation should Prevent British encroachment on Scandinavia and the Baltic; Further, it should guarantee our ore base in Sweden, and Give our Navy and Air Force a wider starting line against Britain.

Adolf Hitler, Directions to the Wehrmacht High Command, 1 March 1940

The subjugation of Denmark and Norway was not originally in Hitler's designs for the conquest and domination of Europe. However, the German Kriegsmarine, smarting from being bottled up at Kiel and Wilhelmshaven during World War I, began to press for just such an operation to secure the Norwegian ports – especially Narvik and Trondheim – soon after the conquest of Poland.

With the full realization that his service was at war with Great Britain once again, Admiral Rolf Carls, the navy's third-ranking officer, promoted the idea in a letter to Grossadmiral Erich Raeder, Commander-in-Chief of the Kriegsmarine. Impressed, Raeder ordered the proposal studied by the Seekriegsleitung (Naval War Staff or SKL) and thought enough of the idea to mention it to Hitler.

On 10 October 1939, in the course of a routine general report to the Führer, Raeder brought up the possibility of securing selected Norwegian ports, especially Trondheim and Narvik, to broaden the operational basis of his service against its primary adversary, the British Royal Navy. Hitler, who had read Vizeadmiral Wolfgang Wegener's 1929 treatise *Die Strategie des Weltkrieges* (*The Strategy of World War*) and understood the strategic significance from the Kriegsmarine's point of view, entertained the idea.

The notion was further encouraged by Vidkun Quisling, formerly the Norwegian Foreign Minister (1931–33). He and his Norwegian Fascist party (the Nasjonal Samling or 'National Union' party) were planning a *coup d'état* and requested the German Army support this uprising with a peaceful occupation to guard against British interference, but this came to very little. When Quisling visited Berlin on 11 December he met with Raeder to seek German support and sanction for his proposed endeavour. Raeder was unimpressed with both Quisling's idea and his lack of indigenous support, but the traitor did mention a disturbing piece of political intelligence: the Norwegian government had decided not to resist any Allied landings if such a situation arose. Dutifully, the German admiral discussed the visit and Quisling's revelation with the Führer the following day. While Raeder would not endorse Quisling or his plan, Hitler readily agreed that British occupation of Norwegian ports would be disastrous – in his words 'unacceptable' – and three days later, after meeting with Quisling himself, he ordered that 'investigations on how to seize Norway … be conducted by a very restricted staff group' at OKW.

German naval auxiliary *Altmark* in Jøssingfjord on 16 February 1940. On board were 299 British merchant seamen captured by the raider *Graf Spee*. (Courtesy Imperial War Museum, London – HU27803)

7

Hitler's anxiety about possible enemy action was high because of the Allies' loud political support for the Finns in their Winter War against the Soviet Union (30 November 1939–12 March 1940). In order to aid Finland, an Allied expeditionary force would have to occupy Narvik in northern Norway and secure the railway running through Sweden to Finland. This would also prevent shipments of Swedish iron ore from Gällivare travelling to Narvik to be loaded onto ships bound for Germany. It was evident from the press in Paris and London that the Allies were considering just such a move, either with the permission of the host nations, Norway and Sweden, or perhaps even without it.

The possibility of unilateral Allied action was considered very real by Hitler and his military staff, and was brought into sharp focus in mid-February by the actions of Captain Philip L. Vian and the destroyer HMS *Cossack*. In a daring and audacious action ordered by First Lord of the Admiralty Winston Churchill himself, the *Cossack* entered Jøssingfjord, near Stavanger, and boarded the German navy auxiliary *Altmark* hiding there. They freed 299 British merchant seamen captured by the 'pocket battleship' *Graf Spee* and spirited them back to Britain amid an outcry of protests from the Norwegian government.

But to Hitler and his staff the fact that the Norwegians could do little more than protest demonstrated just how powerless they were to ward off any real Allied action or, for that matter, defend against a pre-emptive attack by Germany to secure this open flank. To Raeder the possibility of the Royal Navy and Royal Air Force sealing off the North Sea from Scapa Flow, Scotland, to Stavanger, Norway, would create an ironclad blockade that the weaker German fleet could never hope to challenge.

The other persistent anxiety was the threat to the shipments of Swedish iron ore sailing out of Narvik, shipments that were absolutely

The Tribal-class destroyer HMS *Cossack* figured prominently in the Norwegian campaign. It was used to rescue British prisoners from the *Altmark* and, two months later, was heavily engaged – and badly damaged – in the second battle of Narvik. (Courtesy Imperial War Museum, London – FL1657)

essential to the heavily armoured and highly mechanized Nazi war machine. These shipments came from mines at Kiruna in northern Sweden and during the warm months of the year sailed from the port of Luleå on ships steaming down the Gulf of Bothnia and through the Baltic Sea, physically immune to interruption. However, in the winter Luleå was icebound and the shipments were carried by rail across the narrow neck of northern Norway to ice-free Narvik. The German ore ships then steamed down the coast, the route almost completely inside the territorial waters of neutral Norway, passing through a constriction called the Inner Leads off the Stadhavet near Ålesund – immune by virtue of international law from interception and interdiction by British warships. Should the Allies occupy Narvik, the ore shipments would be halted until the ice thawed at Luleå, leaving the great steel mills and armaments factories of Krupp and other Ruhr industries unable to fulfil the requirements for the German Army, as well as the other services.

Therefore, on 27 January 1940, Hitler rejected the OKW's rather sketchy initial planning attempt, called *Studie Nord*, and ordered a new one developed in detail, giving it the cover name *Weserübung* ('Weser [River] Exercise'). A month later he established the operation's objectives and dictated that it must occur before the start of the invasion of France and the Low Countries (codenamed *Fall Gelb* or 'Case Yellow').

Once the decision was made to take Norway, unfortunate Denmark fell into the invasion plan because of the need to secure the staging airfields at Ålborg in northern Jutland. The Luftwaffe high command also favoured the occupation of the little country in order to extend the flank of their air-defence belt further north. At the time, the German air-defence system ended at Helgoland, Sylt and some airfields in Schleswig. It was easy for RAF bombers to circumvent these defensive sites and outflank the air-warning network by flying to the north, threatening the important cities of Hamburg and Kiel, and perhaps even Berlin, with little reaction time for Luftwaffe interceptors.

Thus all three German armed services had an interest in seeing Norway and Denmark brought within the Reich. It is fitting, with these service-centred motivations, that the campaign to do just that was the only real joint offensive conducted by the Germans and the only campaign planned almost exclusively by the Wehrmacht headquarters.

Five days after the *Altmark* incident, Hitler ordered the detailed planning for *Weserübung* to proceed with urgency.

CHRONOLOGY

1939

1 September	Germany invades Poland, beginning World War II.
3 September	Britain and France declare war on Germany.
10 October	Grossadmiral Raeder suggests to Hitler the desirability of securing Trondheim and Narvik as naval/U-boat bases.
30 November	The Soviet Union attacks Finland, starting the Winter War. The Allies begin making plans to aid Finland, through Norway and Sweden if need be.
11 December	Vidkun Quisling meets with Raeder requesting German forces to support his proposed *coup d'état* to prevent British interference – he fails to enlist German support but motivates Hitler to consider action.

1940

27 January	Hitler orders the original staff study for occupying Norway be developed into an operational plan, codenamed *Weserübung*.
16 February	The British destroyer HMS *Cossack* attacks the German navy auxiliary *Altmark* in Jøssingfjord, freeing 299 British seamen and violating Norwegian neutrality.
19 February	Hitler orders the detailed planning for *Weserübung* to proceed with the assignment of units from all three German military services.
3 March	First meeting of the German service chiefs to be informed of and review the plan for *Weserübung*. Hitler decides *Weserübung* will precede *Fall Gelb*.
12 March	Finland accepts Soviet terms, this ends the Winter War.
21 March	In France, the failure to support the Finns causes the government of Daladier to fall; he is replaced as Premier by Paul Reynaud.
28 March	Paul Reynaud attends his first Allied Supreme War Council and supports Winston Churchill's proposal to mine the Norwegian Leads to disrupt German iron ore traffic.
2 April	Hitler meets with operational commanders and reviews plans and preparations – the next day he gives the go-ahead order.
7 April	The German battle squadron and other warships depart their ports, beginning *Weserübung*.
8 April	British destroyers sow mines in Norwegian territorial waters; RN destroyer HMS *Glowworm* is sunk by *Admiral Hipper*. The transport *Rio de Janeiro* is sunk by Polish submarine *Orzel* in the Skagerrak.
9 April	German naval units, infantry divisions, and Luftwaffe squadrons begin the invasion of Denmark and Norway. Denmark capitulates that morning. The Norwegian capital Oslo and the ports of Kristiansand, Stavanger, Bergen, Trondheim and Narvik are occupied.
10 April	First battle of Narvik: two German destroyers and six merchantmen are sunk by RN destroyers for the loss of two ships. Also FAA air attack at Bergen sinks light cruiser *Königsberg*. HM Submarine *Truant* sinks *Karlsruhe*.
13 April	Second battle of Narvik: HMS *Warspite* and nine destroyers eliminate the remaining eight German destroyers while the FAA sinks one U-boat at Narvik.
14 April	The Norwegian 1st Division withdraws into Sweden and is interned. The British 24th (Guards) Brigade begins landing at Harstad.
15 April	The Norwegian 3rd Division surrenders to Germans in southern Norway.

16 April	The British 146th Brigade begins landing at Namsos and moves towards Trondheim.
18 April	The British 148th Brigade begins landing at Åndalsnes and moves to Lillehammer.
22 April	The battle of Lillehammer – the first meeting of German and British troops in combat.
23–24 April	The battle of Vist – the 146th Brigade is driven back to Namsos.
23 April	The British 15th Brigade arrives at Åndalsnes. RAF No. 263 Squadron arrives at Lake Lesjaskog the following day. It is wiped out in two days.
24–25 April	The battle of Kvam, German advance delayed but not stopped.
28 April	The French 27e DBCA arrives in Narvik area and moves to engage GJR 139.
30 April	The Norwegian 4th Division surrenders, ending the fighting in southern Norway.
2 May	The evacuation of Sickleforce from Åndalsnes is complete.
3 May	The evacuation of Mauriceforce from Namsos is complete; the Norwegian 2nd and 5th Divisions surrender to Germans, ending the fighting in central Norway.
6 May	The French 13e DBLE arrive in the Narvik area.
9 May	Polish Podhale Brigade arrives in the Narvik area.
10 May	*Fall Gelb* – German invasion of the West – begins.
11–31 May	The British 24th Brigade is transferred to Bodø and withdrawn.
13 May	The battle of Sedan – Guderian breaks through French defences; French DLCA units engage GJR 139 near Narvik.
20 May	German Panzers reach the English Channel.
26 May	Operation *Dynamo* – the evacuation of the BEF from France – begins.
28 May	French and Norwegian forces retake Narvik.
4 June	Evacuation of Allied forces from Narvik begins; German battle squadron returns to the campaign, steaming unobserved into the Norwegian Sea in Operation *Juno*.
5 June	*Fall Rot* – the final conquest of France – begins.
7 June	The evacuation of Rupertforce from Narvik complete.
8 June	The Norwegian 6th Division surrenders to Germans near Narvik; HMS *Glorious* sunk during Operation *Juno*.
13 June	FAA Skuas attack the *Scharnhorst* at Trondheimfjord.
23 June	*Gneisenau* damaged by HM Submarine *Clyde*.
28 July	The German battle squadron returns to Kiel.

OPPOSING PLANS

THE GERMAN PLAN

Hitler's 1 March directive shifted the German planning effort into higher gear. That directive formally established the operational planning staff, known as Gruppe XXI, and work began to fill in the details of the operation.

The final plan was based on the 'daring actions and surprise execution' of simultaneously delivering the lighter elements of three German army divisions, riding in the crew quarters of almost every available warship, at the five primary seaports of Norway – Oslo, Kristiansand, Bergen, Trondheim and Narvik – while two other divisions crossed the undefended border and small water channels into Denmark.

The greatest threat to the opening moves was expected to be the British naval and air striking forces, especially against the two assault groups bound for Narvik and Trondheim. Covering these groups would be the Kriegsmarine's only battle squadron, the battlecruisers *Gneisenau* and *Scharnhorst*. At the appointed time, the two assault groups would split off for their respective objectives and land specially trained mountain troops at the two strategic points in northern Norway. The lightly armed *Gebirgsjäger* would be reinforced with heavy weapons and supplies brought in by six freighters timed to arrive shortly after the assault elements.

At sea, the whole operation was to be screened by 28 U-boats, about two thirds of those available, stationed in lines in the North Sea and off the Norwegian coast.

Oslo was to be taken by an airborne assault on Fornebu Airfield and seaborne infantry from another heavy *Marine Gruppe*. Following the landings, the remaining German cargo ships were to follow to ferry substantial reinforcements across the Kattegat. These would advance outwards from Oslo to subjugate the southern part of the country.

In addition to the air assaults the Luftwaffe was to provide defensive air cover, anti-shipping attacks and air support for the ground forces. Once airbases were secure the Luftwaffe was to mount an air bridge to provide the most critical elements for the expanding ground forces. Fighters were to arrive in Norway to establish local air superiority and dive-bombers were to follow to drive off the British fleet.

Denmark was to be overrun in a simultaneous ground assault rolling across Jutland and an airborne assault to secure the critical Ålborg airfields, as well as a surprise attack by infantry forces in Copenhagen harbour disgorged from naval auxiliaries that were to steam into port during the night.

The German plan was exceedingly complex, requiring close coordination and precise timing by almost all elements of the various units

The primary instigator and the main driving force of Operation *Weserübung* was Grossadmiral Erich Raeder, commander of the Kriegsmarine. (Courtesy Imperial War Museum, London – A14906)

to secure the initial objectives. It was also intricately interdependent, requiring that each force – whether land, sea or air – accomplish its objective in a timely manner or risk the failure of the whole enterprise.

THE ALLIES' COUNTERPLAN

The Danes fully realized that, because of their vulnerable frontier and meagre means, defence against a determined invasion by their powerful neighbour to the south was impossible and instead relied on the assurances of the German–Danish Non-Aggression Treaty of 1939. Signed on 31 May in Berlin, the document confirmed 'the existing friendly relations of neighbourship' and the Danish government took extraordinary steps to prevent providing the Germans with any provocation for invasion.

The Norwegians spurned Nazi overtures to sign a similar treaty and the army made plans to meet attacks from either Germany or the Soviet Union. But, since these antagonists would have to force their way through Denmark and Sweden respectively, the time necessary to mobilize the army was expected to be available. Since the Royal Navy 'ruled the waves' the high seas were not considered a viable avenue of approach for Germany. This assumption resulted in the defences being strongest in the south – to meet a crossing of the Skagerrak and Kattegat – with only a few vital points being defended up the 3,418km-long coastline.

The Allied plan to counter a German invasion began as a proposal to save the Finns from defeat by the Soviets. This was short lived, however, for the Finns surrendered before the Allies could decide what to do. In France this lack of action toppled the Daladier government and brought the more aggressive Paul Reynaud to power.

In his first meeting with the Allied Supreme War Council, held in London on 28 March, Reynaud was briefed by Churchill on his pet proposal, to lay mines in the Norwegian Leads to disrupt the German

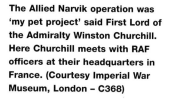

The Allied Narvik operation was 'my pet project' said First Lord of the Admiralty Winston Churchill. Here Churchill meets with RAF officers at their headquarters in France. (Courtesy Imperial War Museum, London – C368)

iron ore shipments from Narvik. Unlike his predecessor and the timid, vacillating British Prime Minister, Reynaud readily agreed and the operation was planned under the code name *Wilfred*, so named by Churchill after a children's cartoon character because of its supposedly 'minor and innocent' nature.

An anticipated consequence to this neutrality-violating operation was that the Germans might invade Norway to secure the route for their ore supply. For this contingency Plan *R.4* was devised, which allocated an infantry brigade to occupy Narvik, and battalions to hold Stavanger, Bergen and Trondheim. The expedition was to be launched as soon as 'the Germans set foot on Norwegian soil, or [when] there is clear evidence that they intend to do so'. For fast transport across the North Sea, the battalions for Stavanger and Bergen were to be embarked upon the four heavy cruisers of the 1st Cruiser Squadron at Rosyth on the Firth of Forth in Scotland. The forces bound for Narvik and Trondheim were to follow in slower, traditional transports.

Despite its reactive nature, Plan *R.4* assumed British and French troops would arrive ahead of the enemy and not have to conduct an opposed landing. These forces were to hold the ports against German amphibious assaults while the Norwegian Army defended in the south.

In the final analysis Plan *R.4* was naive and amateurish in comparison with its Wehrmacht counterpart. It was totally reactive in nature – forfeiting the initiative to the enemy from the very outset – and its troop strengths were pitifully small. While the Germans thought in terms of divisions, the Allies allocated mere battalions. If nothing else, the absence of any planned air cover – having none of the four RN aircraft carriers available and no RAF fighter squadrons assigned to the expeditionary force – clearly indicates its inadequacy of thought and the inevitability of failure.

OPPOSING COMMANDERS

THE GERMANS

The German military officers chosen to lead their forces in *Weserübung* are uniformly characterized by the almost perfect match of their training, background and previous experience to the requirements of the daunting task being undertaken.

To command the overall operation, General Nikolaus von Falkenhorst's name was nominated to Hitler on 19 February. Von Falkenhorst had been born in Breslau in 1885 and began life as Nikolaus von Jastrzembski. However, early in his military career he forsook this decidedly un-German name for the more romantic and Wagnerian 'Falkenhorst' or 'falcon's eyrie'. By the end of World War I he was the operations officer for General von der Goltz's Ostseedivision in Finland where he had worked with the Imperial Navy – two obvious advantages for the Scandinavian adventure being planned.

In the Polish campaign he commanded XXI Armee Korps, defeating the Pomorze Army on the lower Vistula. The initial meetings with Hitler on 21 February went well and, after von Falkenhorst returned that evening with a concept of operations that Hitler liked, the Führer entrusted *Weserübung* to him, emphasizing the critical need for secrecy.

To command the forces invading and occupying Denmark, Generalleutnant Leonhard Kaupisch was selected. Kaupisch was an experienced artillery officer and World War I veteran who had already retired twice as a general, the first time in 1935. On the eve of the Nazi invasion of Poland he was recalled the second time to command the task force that drove across the Danzig Corridor. Afterwards, as army units were hustled to the west, he was left in charge of a corps HQ without forces, called Höheres Kommando XXXI, in East Prussia.

Generalleutnant Eduard Dietl commanded the mountain troops headed for Narvik. Dietl was a small, wiry, leather-tough Bavarian mountaineer who had made a name for himself within the Nazi party in the 1920s, participating in the famous Munich Beer Hall Putsch. Hitler, recognizing the propaganda value on the home front of glamorous military figures, chose Dietl as one of his two Nazi heroes – 'one in the sun and one in the snow' (Rommel became the other). Dietl had substance as well as style and commanded the 99th Alpine Regiment in the *Anschluß* of Austria and the conquest of Poland. Promoted to *Generalleutnant* on 1 April, he was given command of the 3.Gebirgs-Division and put in charge of the all-important Narvik expedition.

Because of the illness of the German fleet commander, Admiral Wilhelm Marschall, Vizeadmiral Günther Lütjens led the naval forces assigned and personally commanded the German battlecruiser squadron. Lütjens' career had been strong and progressive, commanding the

A corps commander in the Polish campaign, General Nikolaus von Falkenhorst had extensive World War I experience in Scandinavia and had worked closely with the Imperial German Navy. (Bundesarchiv Bild 183-2006-0529-501)

Nazi 'poster child'
Generalleutnant Eduard Dietl
was one of Hitler's favourites.
He commanded the 3.Gebirgs-
Division and was in charge of the
Narvik branch of the operation.
(Bundesarchiv Bild 146-1984-
019-20)

Kriegsmarine's torpedo boats before being named *Führer der Zerstörer* for the Polish campaign. Promoted afterwards to *Vizeadmiral* and Commander-in-Chief Reconnaissance Forces (cruisers, torpedo boats and minesweepers) on the eve of the Norwegian campaign, he would lead the largest contingent of German warships to sail from Wilhelmshaven since the ignominious steaming of the High Seas Fleet to Scapa Flow following the Armistice of World War I.

Generalleutnant Hans Ferdinand Geisler's Fliegerkorps X was selected to provide the much-needed air support for this ambitious operation. A former naval officer himself, Geisler was a perfect choice for commanding air forces supporting maritime operations. When the Luftwaffe absorbed all elements of the navy's air arm in 1933 he became an air force officer, continuing to rise in rank until, six years later – as a *Generalmajor* – became responsible for anti-shipping operations. His Fliegerdivision 10 was formed on 5 September 1939 with two bomber groups and, six weeks later, expanded and upgraded to Fliegerkorps X.

THE NEUTRALS

The 70-year-old Danish monarch, King Christian X, was also the commander-in-chief of the Danish armed forces. Commanding the army was General Wilhelm W. Prior and the navy chief was Vice-Admiral H. Rechnitzer.

Norway's King Håkon VII, born in 1872 as Prince Charles of Denmark, was the brother of Denmark's Christian X. He had been elected king of Norway following the granting of that nation's independence from Sweden in 1905. A well respected and benevolent monarch of a peaceful, industrious people, King Håkon also possessed the will and strength of character to oppose the subjugation of his adopted nation.

The commander of the Norwegian Army was Generalmajor Kristian Låke. At the age of 65, Låke was lazy, lethargic and concerned only about his own personal comfort. While perhaps an adequate administrator in organizing the army, he proved unfit to command and King Håkon quickly replaced him with the dynamic and industrious Oberst Otto Ruge, the Inspector General (IG) of Infantry. Admiral Henry Diesen commanded the small Norwegian Navy.

THE ALLIES

After an aborted attempt at deploying the British battalions to Norway under the overall command of Admiral Sir Edward Evans, Churchill passed the job to Admiral William Boyle, the 12th Earl of Cork and Orrery. Short of stature and ramrod straight, Adm. Boyle was a dynamic and dedicated naval officer with an exemplary career. Coming from a rather impoverished aristocratic family, he joined the Royal Navy in 1886 at the age of 11 and progressed brilliantly through the ranks, commanding warships from torpedo boat destroyers to battleships by World War I. In 1917 he was given command of the new battlecruiser HMS *Repulse* and led her in action against German cruisers in the battle of Heligoland Bight that November.

Following World War I he continued to rise in rank until he was named Commander-in-Chief of the Home Fleet in March 1933. While in command, he became the 12th Earl of Cork and Orrery in 1934, inheriting the title from his cousin. Lord Cork, as he was known thereafter, was finally promoted to Admiral of the Fleet in 1938 and retired at the age of 66 at the end of June the following year.

However, with the opening rounds of World War II, Churchill recalled him to service in the Admiralty as an advisor and when assigning him the task of overall command of the Norwegian expedition he encouraged Lord Cork to 'act with all promptitude … [in order to] … turn the enemy out of Narvik.'

By virtue of his rank, as Flag Officer Narvik, Lord Cork was also responsible for the Allied operation. But initially he commanded only the Royal Navy elements involved (reinforced with a few French and Polish warships). His ground forces commander was Major-General Pierse J. Mackesy, commander of the 49th (West Riding) Division. Mackesy was a distinguished commander, having proved himself in the military mission to South Russia in 1919–20 and while commanding a brigade in Palestine before the war. He was, among many officers of his generation, a disciple of B. H. Liddell-Hart's 'indirect approach' as a means of avoiding the staggering casualties experienced in World War I. Additionally, armed with orders from General Sir Edmund Ironside, Chief of the Imperial General Staff, with express instructions first to establish a base from which to advance upon Narvik, he insisted on a deliberate and incremental approach to securing the objective.

Lord Cork, on the other hand, favoured an immediate storming of Narvik using both naval and ground forces. Ostensibly in charge of the entire operation, Lord Cork's actual authority ended where Maj. Gen. Mackesy's began. Even elevating Lord Cork to command of all forces on 21 April failed to resolve these diametrically opposed views on how the campaign should proceed. Consequently Lord Cork petitioned London for the replacement of Mackesy.

As his new ground force commander, the tall, athletic Major-General Claude J. E. Auchinleck was a fitting choice. Commissioned in 1904 into the 62nd Punjab Regiment, he distinguished himself during World War I in action in Egypt, Aden and Mesopotamia, winning the Distinguished Service Order (DSO). Between the wars he commanded the Peshawar Brigade and led them in two successful campaigns on India's north-west frontier. Promoted to major-general in 1936, he was recalled to Britain and named commander of the British Expeditionary Force (BEF) IV Corps once World War II began. Reassigned to the Narvik campaign in early May, much was expected of this imaginative and sometimes unconventional leader. However, by the time he arrived there was little he could do to change the Allied approach to recapturing Narvik.

Tactical control of land operations would eventually be passed to the French Général de brigade Marie Antoine E. Béthouart. Graduating from St Cyr military academy in 1912, he began his career with the French Alpine troops, being wounded three times in World War I. Dynamic and determined to beat the Germans, he was promoted to brigadier on 15 April and given command of the 1ère Division Légère de Chasseurs, formed specifically for the Norwegian campaign. Béthouart easily proved to be the ablest commander on the Allied side.

Retired Admiral of the Fleet William Boyle, 12th Earl of Cork and Orrery, was recalled to active service by Churchill as an advisor, but soon found himself in charge of the Allies' Narvik expedition. (UK National Portrait Gallery Neg. Nr. X67909)

A successful commander in Russia and Palestine, Major-General P. J. Mackesy favoured the deliberate but indirect approach in order to avoid high casualty figures. (UK National Portrait Gallery Neg. Nr. X165819)

OPPOSING FORCES

GERMAN FORCES ASSIGNED

Ground forces

Since *Weserübung* could not be allowed to prejudice the upcoming, all-important invasion of the West, the ground units initially assigned to Gruppe XXI were limited to seven infantry divisions, one mountain division, a battalion of paratroopers and a handful of old training and experimental tanks.

For the subjugation of Denmark, Höheres Kommando XXXI consisted mainly of the 170. and 198.Infanterie Divisionen. On the left flank, racing up the west coast of Denmark to relieve the paratroopers and air-landed infantry at Ålborg's two airfields, was the 11.Schützenbrigade (mot) reinforced with one of three motorized machine-gun battalions. Two light Panzer companies from the ad hoc Panzer Abteilung 40, consisting of 46 PzKpfw IB and II light tanks, also stiffened the invading infantry.

For the invasion of Norway, Gen. von Falkenhorst had the equivalent of two army corps – a total of six divisions. In the first wave were portions of two infantry divisions, the 69.Infanterie Division landing at Bergen and the 163.Infanterie Division at Oslo, as well as the 3.Gebirgs-Division bound for Narvik and Trondheim. The second wave consisted of three infantry divisions reinforcing the ground advance from Oslo.

While Norway could never be considered 'good tank country', the inclusion of the few experimental NbFz B tanks proved to be a fortuitous decision by the German planners. The Norwegian Army had no anti-tank weapons at all. (Bundesarchiv Bild 101I-761-221-N-06)

The advance into the interior would initially be supported by one company of 20 light tanks and later by one platoon of experimental pre-war Neubaufahrzeug B heavy tanks. These 35-ton, multi-turret 'land battleships' were designed to work closely with the infantry, supporting them with their coaxially mounted 75mm and 37mm cannon in the main turret and two small machine-gun turrets fore and aft.

Assigned to the crucial Narvik branch of the operation was Gen.Lt. Dietl's 3.Gebirgs-Division. Formed in 1938 from units of the Austrian 5. and 7.Gebirgs-Divisionen, these elite mountain troops would definitely be the furthest from home. The unit was composed of two 3,000-man *Gebirgsjäger* regiments, a four *Ableitungen* artillery regiment and battalion-sized reconnaissance, anti-tank, engineer (pioneer) and signals units. The division's Gebirgsjäger Regiment 139 was to secure Narvik while GJR 138 landed at Trondheim. The pack howitzers and heavier guns of Gebirgs-Artillerie Regiment 112 were to follow by slower sea transport.

In support Gen. von Falkenhorst had four batteries of 100mm guns and two more of 150mm field pieces. Finally, the ground commanders could expect reinforcement by the three motorized machine-gun battalions and two companies of light tanks from Denmark, once the occupation of that tiny nation was complete.

Kriegsmarine

The brainchild of the Kriegsmarine, *Weserübung* required all that the German Navy had available. Compared with the RN's Home Fleet, these means were severely limited and the planners and commanders had to make the very best of what they had.

The most powerful combat element was the German battlecruiser squadron consisting of the near-twin *Gneisenau* and *Scharnhorst*. Called *Schlachtschiffe* (battleships) in Germany, they displaced 37,800 tons each and were heavily armoured but had limited hitting power with their three triple 28cm turrets. Fast, with a top speed of 31 knots, they could outrun British battleships and battlecruisers alike.

Supplementing these two capital ships was the 14,290-ton former *Panzerschiff Deutschland*, now named *Lützow*. Referred to as 'pocket battleships' by the contemporary press and many history books, this type

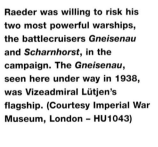

Raeder was willing to risk his two most powerful warships, the battlecruisers *Gneisenau* and *Scharnhorst*, in the campaign. The *Gneisenau*, seen here under way in 1938, was Vizeadmiral Lütjen's flagship. (Courtesy Imperial War Museum, London – HU1043)

had been formally reclassified as 'heavy cruisers' to confuse enemy intelligence, but are more aptly called armoured cruisers. Small but powerfully armed with two 28cm triple turrets, they too were speedy, capable of 28 knots.

More conventionally, the German navy also had two modern and powerful heavy cruisers. The *Admiral Hipper* (18,600 tons) was commissioned in April 1939 and the brand new *Blücher* (18,695 tons) had just completed its trials immediately prior to *Weserübung*. With the latest in fire-control equipment and mounting eight 20.3cm guns in four dual turrets, they were arguably the best heavy cruisers of the day. Additionally, the Kriegsmarine had six light cruisers counting the obsolescent 6,990-ton *Emden* (1925), which was of a pre-World War I design and served primarily as a training ship. Far more modern were the three 'K-class' *Spähkreuzer* ('scouting cruisers') – the *Karlsruhe* (1929), *Königsberg* (1929) and *Köln* (1930) – which were 6,750-ton vessels mounting nine 15cm guns in three triple turrets. The improved *Leipzig* (8,425 tons) and *Nürnberg* (9,040 tons) were undergoing extensive repairs, having been hit by torpedoes from HMS *Salmon* in December 1939.

During the economic depression of the early 1930s, the German Navy focused its limited resources on cruisers and did not address the need for robust, ocean-going *Zerstörer* (destroyers) until 1934, when building began for a total of 22 in three batches (*Z.1–Z.4*: 2,232 tons; *Z.5–Z.16*: 2,270 tons; *Z.17–Z.22*: 2,411 tons). Mounting five 12.7cm guns and eight torpedo tubes these were excellent warships for this class, superior in size, armament and speed to their British opponents, but there were only 20 available.

Not being an expeditionary-minded service compared with the US and Royal Navies, the Kriegsmarine lacked troop transports, military cargo vessels and assault craft. It was therefore dependent on merchant ships and ocean liners to transport reinforcing personnel and heavy *matériel* to the objective ports. However, it had a substantial coastal defence force with significant numbers of torpedo boats (small World War I-era destroyer-like vessels), mine warfare craft, patrol vessels and fast torpedo-armed attack craft called *Schnellboote* ('fast boats' or S-boats). The heavy requirements of the invasion operation meant even these craft would be pressed into service as escorts and transports.

Luftwaffe units

Fliegerkorps X, the Luftwaffe's specialized anti-shipping command, provided the air component of the Wehrmacht's only joint offensive force. Assigned directly to the Oberbefehlshaber der Luftwaffe (Luftwaffe High Command or ObdL), it consisted of two *Geschwader* ('wings', each with three groups) of He 111s and a third of Ju 88s, plus Kampfgruppe 100, equipped with the experimental X-Gerät radio-navigation and bombing system.

These units had ranged across the North Sea with impunity and had struck the RN's anchorages in the Firth of Forth and at Scapa Flow on several occasions. While no warships had been sunk, the regularity of the strikes convinced the Admiralty to move the Home Fleet to the west coast until local defences could be strengthened. Additionally, the command sank 32 small coastal cargo ships and fishing trawlers (36,190 tons total) and five RN minesweepers along the eastern coast of Britain.

By April 1940, these courageous, determined and resourceful Luftwaffe crews were well experienced in anti-shipping operations.

Two groups of Bf 110C twin-engine fighters reinforced them for long-range escort, along with one group of Bf 109E single-engine fighters for the defence of captured airfields and one group of long-range Ju 87R Stuka dive-bombers, plus a few battlefield observation and long-range reconnaissance squadrons. These brought the command up to 527 combat aircraft, of which 317 were bombers.

Additionally, Fliegerkorps X was required to conduct the first combat use of paratroopers and airborne assault, followed by establishing an extensive aerial bridge across the waters to Norway. For the first, three groups from the 7.Fliegerdivision's Kampfgeschwader zur besonderen Verwendung 1 (battle wing for special duties) were temporarily assigned to drop paratroopers and deliver follow-up infantry units. For the second, every available transport from Lufthansa and the Luftwaffe's multi-engine and instrument flying schools were formed into seven transport groups (KGrzbV 101 through 107). Six of these were equipped with the venerable Junkers Ju 52/3m tri-motor transports but one (KGrzbV 105) contained 20 four-engine transports (Ju 90s, the new FW 200 and one old Junkers G 38) from Lufthansa, many still in their airline livery. An eighth (KGrzbV 108), made up of 27 transport floatplanes, was for use at objectives that had no airfields but were accessible by water landings. The 40 squadrons totalled some 533 aircraft, the largest airlift armada yet employed in warfare.

One battalion of paratroopers – all that could be spared for the upcoming *Fall Gelb* operation – was supplied from Fliegerdivision 7. I Bataillon of Fallschirmjäger Regiment 1 (I/FJR 1), which was the most experienced paratroop unit available, having trained for parachute assault operations since 1936. It consisted of four companies and a headquarters element of similar size.

DANISH ARMED FORCES

By 1937 it was apparent to the Danish government that at least a strengthened military force was needed to deter the belligerent intentions of their southern neighbour. The Defence Act of that year expanded the small army, establishing a general headquarters, two

The Norwegian Army air arm would meet the German air assault with a single squadron of Gloster Gladiator biplane fighters based at Fornebu Airfield, the primary target of the Luftwaffe's air assault operation. (Postma Collection, TP1721)

divisions – one for Jutland and one for Zealand – and the Bornholm garrison; restructured the air arm; and established anti-aircraft, engineer and transportation supporting units.

The two divisions totalled seven infantry regiments, two cavalry, the Life Guards (the king's palace guard) and three field artillery regiments, plus supporting units. However, the regiments were actually small administrative staffs responsible for the training of the 6,600 conscripts each year; consequently, they were severely under strength. The two divisions were supported by the army's aviation branch (Hærens Flyvertropper, or Army Aviation Troops) consisting of two fighter squadrons equipped with Gloster Gauntlet biplanes and new Fokker D.XXI monoplanes, and two of Fokker C.V observation biplanes. The entire air arm was based at Værløse airfield near Copenhagen.

The Danish Navy was based at Copenhagen and had 1,500 men working some 58 vessels, most of them old and outmoded. The most formidable warships were two old coastal defence ships. The most modern were three small torpedo boats completed in the early 1930s and four new, though small, submarines. The navy had its own air arm (Marinen Flyvevæesenets, or Naval Flying Service) composed of two squadron-sized *luftflotilles* (air flotillas), one of ancient Heinkel H.E.8 floatplanes based at Copenhagen and a fighter unit with elderly Hawker Nimrod Mk. II biplanes stationed at Avnø.

NORWEGIAN ARMED FORCES

Having emerged from its union with Sweden in 1905, Norway was a sparsely populated country with few resources and no real martial or naval tradition. Consequently the nation adopted a territorial army concept, utilizing trained reservists to fill its ranks.

The country was divided into six military districts, headquartered at Halden, Oslo, Kristiansand, Bergen, Trondheim and Harstad, each organized to field a division upon mobilization. Norwegian divisions were infantry formations comprising a staff, two or three infantry regiments and either an artillery regiment or a mountain artillery battalion. They possessed no armour or anti-tank weapons since it was believed the rugged terrain precluded mechanized operations.

Infantry regiments had a strength of 3,750 men supported by organic machine-gun battalions. Horse-mounted cavalry regiments or bicycle/ski scout companies were used for reconnaissance. Horse-drawn Kongsberg 120mm howitzers and Ehrhardt 75mm field guns provided artillery support.

Learning quickly that aircraft could overcome the vast distances involved in defending the nation the Hæerens Flyvevåpen (Army Air Service) had developed into an effective army cooperation force using now-obsolete Fokker C.V biplanes. They were organized into three reconnaissance 'flights' (called Speidevingen) located in southern, central and northern Norway.

Additionally, to defend the capital the Hæerens Flyvevåpen had a single fighter unit (Jagervingen, or fighter flight) with nine Gloster Gladiator biplanes based at Fornebu Airfield near Oslo. Additionally a light bomber unit (Bombervingen, or bomber flight) had recently been formed with four twin-engine Caproni Ca.310 light bombers and eight Fokker C.V-Es. Normally based at Kjeller, near Oslo, this unit was deployed to the new, modern Sola airfield at Stavanger.

The Norwegian Navy was a small force designed to defend the most important ports and harbours along the extensive coastline. The two most heavily armed ships were a pair of ancient coastal defence ships (built before 1900), the *Norge* and *Eidsvold* (4,166 tons), mounting two 21cm guns in single turrets fore and aft, with secondary batteries of six 15cm and eight 76mm guns. These were deployed to Narvik at the first suspicion of the German invasion.

The navy's seven small destroyers – four of them modern 597-ton vessels armed with three 4in. and one 40mm guns, and two torpedo tubes – were scattered between Oslo and Narvik. Filling in the gaps were 17 World War I-vintage torpedo boats, nine small coastal submarines, eight minesweepers, ten minelayers and nine patrol boats. Additionally there were 49 craft pressed into service as patrol vessels.

To help cover Norway's extensive coastline, the naval air arm (Marinens Flyvevåpen, or Naval Air Service) had three squadron-sized composite units based at Horton (the main naval base near Oslo), Bergen and Tromsø. These were equipped primarily with the indigenous Høver M.F.11 reconnaissance biplanes and new Heinkel He 115A twin-engine torpedo-bombers. With these flying units the Marinens Flyvevåpen conducted frequent long-ranging patrols over Norwegian territorial waters and out across the North Sea, vainly seeking to enforce Norway's precious but tenuous neutrality.

The Norwegians had seven small but capable destroyers, seen here on manoeuvres. This photo, published by the Norwegian Information Service to demonstrate the strength of their navy, was sent to British media the morning the Germans were invading. (Courtesy Imperial War Museum, London – HU91801)

ALLIED EXPEDITIONARY FORCES

By the time Plan *R.4* was approved, the British Army had deployed 11½ of its 14 divisions to the BEF in France. The remaining forces were primarily infantry battalions – both regular and those of the volunteer and reservist-manned Territorial Army – formed into brigades for combat employment.

The British contingent destined for Norway was composed primarily of battalions of Territorial Army reservists gathered into brigades. Here they wait on the quayside to board their troopship. (Courtesy Imperial War Museum, London – N3)

Supplementing the British were six battalions of *Chasseurs alpins*. These French mountain troops were the best trained and most effective of the Allied units for fighting the German *Gebirgsjäger* around Narvik. (Courtesy Imperial War Museum, London – N159)

Four of these, including the 24th (Guards) Brigade from Maj. Gen. Mackesy's 49th Division, were designated for dispatch to Norway.

In 1940 British brigades were composed of three 813-man infantry battalions and an anti-tank company of nine Hotchkiss 25mm guns. A support company provided carrier, 3in. mortar, light AA, pioneer, signals and administrative platoons. Normally amply supported with artillery, the brigades slated for Norway only had the 203rd Field Battery/51st Field Regiment, Royal Artillery and its dozen 25-pdr field pieces.

Supplementing the British brigades, the French *Chasseurs alpins* were singularly appropriate to face the German *Gebirgsjäger* in the rocky heights of northern Norway. They were the only elements in the Allied forces trained, equipped and accustomed to mountain campaigning in wintry conditions. For the Norwegian expedition six *Chasseurs alpins* battalions were organized into two *demi-brigades* of the 1ère Division Légère de Chasseurs Alpins.

A *demi-brigade* was a uniquely French formation made up of two or three normally independent battalions. A *Chasseurs alpins* battalion comprised a headquarters section, three rifle companies and a machine-gun company. The rifle companies contained 190 men each, and the machine-gun company supplied four machine-gun sections and one gun section of two 25mm A/T guns and two 81mm mortars.

The *Chasseurs alpins* would be complemented by a *demi-brigade* of the *Légion étrangère*, the 13e Demi-Brigade de Légion Étrangère (DBLE), made up of two infantry battalions. They were also supported by an independent colonial artillery group containing three four-gun batteries of 1897-pattern 75mm field pieces, a motorcycle reconnaissance element and an independent tank company with 15 Hotchkiss H-39 light tanks.

Also sent from France was the Polish army-in-exile's 1st Independent Podhale ('Highland') Brigade. Some 35,000 Polish soldiers had escaped the destruction of their army and made their way to France, and a portion of these organized the Podhale Brigade under Gen. Zygmunt Bohusz-Szysko. Carrying on the traditions and lineage of the Polish Army's highland divisions of the Carpathian region of southern Poland they were the first to be re-equipped by the French.

The brigade was organized along French Army lines, consisting of two *demi-brigades*, each with two battalions. Although it was intended they be equipped like the *Chasseurs alpins*, alongside whom they were to fight, shortages of mountaineer equipment resulted in them being issued with a varied selection of French uniforms, equipment and weapons.

Royal Navy Home Fleet

The Royal Navy's Home Fleet began the war as one of the most powerful modern armadas afloat. On the day Britain declared war on Hitler's Nazi Germany, the fleet boasted five battleships and two battlecruisers, two aircraft carriers, 13 cruisers, 17 destroyers and 20 submarines. However, losses, damage and reassignment reduced the battle line to three battleships and the pair of battlecruisers. These were the battleships HMS *Rodney*, a modern 33,300-ton vessel and Adm. Sir Charles M. Forbes' flagship, and two old Jutland veterans, the 31,585-ton HMS *Valiant* and 31,816-ton HMS *Warspite*, with the latter scheduled to return to the Mediterranean on 7 April. There were also the 30,750-ton battlecruisers

The battlecruiser HMS *Renown* would be the first British capital ship to meet its German counterpart in battle since World War I. Heavily modified and up-armoured, the World War I veteran was more than a match for its adversaries. (United States Naval Institute with Imperial War Museum Permission)

HMS *Renown* and *Repulse*. While both of these were also World War I veterans, they had been modernized and considerably uparmoured to reduce the type's vulnerability that had caused such shocking losses at Jutland.

Recognizing the aeroplane's increased effectiveness against warships, the RN had converted six old 4,290-ton C-Class cruisers to AA escorts. Led by HMS *Curlew* in 1935 this class mounted four Mk. XIX twin-barrel turrets of 4in. high-angle, dual-purpose (anti-ship as well as anti-aircraft) guns. These could be elevated to near vertical and were directed by two HA controllers to meet attacking aircraft with a barrage of quick-firing, high-explosive fire.

The RN was fortunate that it had the budget to build a flotilla of destroyers each year from 1928 to 1939. Most of these (A through H Classes) averaged about 1,350 tons standard displacement and culminated in the H-Class armed with four Mk. IX 4.7in. guns in single mountings. The next class – 18 considerably larger Tribal-Class ships – displaced 1,855 tons and carried eight Mk. XIX dual-purpose 4.7in. guns in four twin-gun turrets. Although lighter than their German opponents they represented a much-needed improvement in hitting power, with twice the number of fast firing guns.

The RN also had a great advantage in its submarine service, commanded by the keen and dynamic World War I veteran submariner Vice-Admiral Max K. Horton. Suspecting, in advance of almost all his colleagues, that a German invasion of Norway was in the offing, he positioned 12 of his boats (including two French and one Polish) in the waters between the invader and its northern victim. Convinced that *Wilfred* would precipitate this expected reaction, he dispatched another six submarines to these areas on 7 April to interdict the German assault forces crossing by sea.

The Home Fleet's greatest deficiency was what it would need the most – air cover. Of the two aircraft carriers assigned at the beginning of the war, HMS *Furious* was in dry dock undergoing refit and HMS *Ark Royal* was in the Mediterranean undergoing training. The former typically embarked 30 aircraft in two torpedo-spotter-reconnaissance squadrons flying Fairey Swordfish TSR Mk. Is. The latter was the RN's most modern vessel, normally carrying 54 aircraft in two Skua and three Swordfish squadrons. At the time these units were stationed at Hatston airfield in the Orkneys awaiting the return of their ships.

Despite the depletion of the battle squadron, Adm. Forbes' fleet still had a decided advantage over the entire Kriegsmarine and, when including the cruiser force based at Rosyth, RN forces facing the North Sea were overpowering. It would be a matter of how they were used.

Royal Air Force

Leaving the naval threat in the North Sea to the Royal Navy, the RAF was poorly positioned for the Norwegian campaign. Its Bomber and Fighter Commands naturally concentrated their offensive and defensive might in south-east England for proximity to the European continent and the Third Reich. Coastal Command was spread thinly, mostly facing the Western Approaches from south-west England to search for U-boats. The remainder of their forces was based in Scotland, but few could reach Norway even from there.

Coastal Command's 18 Group was mainly responsible for maritime reconnaissance and convoy protection in the North Sea. Of its four seaplane squadrons, only No. 204 Squadron at Sullom Voe in the Shetland Islands was a capable unit, equipped with the excellent Short Sunderland four-engine flying boat. The group also had three squadrons of Lockheed Hudsons – a makeshift maritime patrol bomber developed from the Super Electra series of commercial passenger planes.

Eventually, to provide fighter cover for the Allied ground forces in Norway two Fighter Command squadrons were called upon. The first to be called was No. 263 Squadron. This new unit was formed at Bristol's Filton airfield with Gloster Gladiator biplanes and had just become operational in December 1939. Its members had no idea they would be involved in forthcoming events until the evening of 9 April when they were ordered to collect their Artic equipment and stores.

Reinforcing them later would be No. 46 Squadron, a Hurricane unit that had already tasted combat: late on 21 October they shot down four (of nine) slow, ungainly He 115A floatplane torpedo bombers approaching a coastal convoy. The unit subsequently moved to Acklington, from where it patrolled against incursions and anti-shipping strikes by Fliegerkorps X.

Against the might of the Luftwaffe – 317 bombers – the RAF planned on deploying 36 fighters. The inability to maintain even local air superiority over their own ground forces doomed the Allied campaign before it ever began.

ORDERS OF BATTLE

GERMAN FORCES

Heer

Gruppe XXI – Gen. Nikolaus von Falkenhorst

First wave

69.Infanterie Division – Gen.Maj. Hermann Tittel
Infanterie Regt. 159
Infanterie Regt. 193
Infanterie Regt. 236
Artillerie Regt. 169
169 Aufklärungs-Abt.
169 Panzerabwehr-Abt.
Pionier-Bn. 169
169 Nachrichten-Abt.

163.Infanterie Division – Gen.Maj. Erwin Engelbrecht
Infanterie Regt. 307
Infanterie Regt. 310
Infanterie Regt. 324
Artillerie Regt. 234 (+)
234 Aufklärungs-Abt.
234 Panzerabwehr-Abt.
Pionier-Bn. 234
234 Nachrichten-Abt.

3.Gebirgs-Division – Gen.Lt. Eduard Dietl
Gebirgsjäger Regt. 138
Gebirgsjäger Regt. 139
Gebirgs-Artillerie Regt. 112
Radfahrer Bn. 68
Gebirgs-Panzerjäger Bn. 48
Gebirgs-Pionier Bn. 83
Gebirgs-Nachrichten Bn. 68

I Bataillon(-)/Fallschirmjäger Regiment 1 (Luftwaffe)

Second wave

181.Infanterie Division – Gen.Maj. Kurt Woytasch
Fusilier Regt. 334
Infanterie Regt. 349
Infanterie Regt. 359 (-)
Artillerie Regt. 222
222 Aufklärungs-Abt.
222 Panzerabwehr-Abt.
Pionier-Bn. 222
222 Nachrichten-Abt.

196.Infanterie Division – Gen.Lt. Richard Pellengahr
Infanterie Regt. 340
Infanterie Regt. 345
Infanterie Regt. 362
Artillerie Regt. 223
223 Aufklärungs-Abt.
223 Panzerabwehr-Abt.
Pionier-Bn. 223
223 Nachrichten-Abt.

214.Infanterie Division – Gen.Maj. Max Horn
Infanterie Regt. 355
Infanterie Regt. 367
Infanterie Regt. 388
Artillerie Regt. 214
214 Aufklärungs-Abt.
214 Panzerabwehr-Abt.
Pionier-Bn. 214
214 Nachrichten-Abt.

Reserve
3.Kompanie/Panzer-Abt. 40 – 20 PzKpfw I/II light tanks
One Zug ('Panzerzug Horstmann') of three NbFz B heavy tanks
Artillerie-Abt 730 (motorized)
169.Infanterie Division

FOR DENMARK
Höheres Kommando XXXI – Gen.Lt. Leonhard Kaupisch

170.Infanterie Division – Gen.Maj. Walter Wittke
Infanterie Regt. 391
Infanterie Regt. 399
Infanterie Regt. 401 (-)
Artillerie Regt. 240
Panzerabwehr-Kp. 240
Pionier-Bn. 240
240 Nachrichten-Abt.

198.Infanterie Division – Gen.Maj. Otto Roettig
Infanterie Regt. 305
Infanterie Regt. 308
Infanterie Regt. 326
Artillerie Regt. 235
Panzerabwehr-Kp. 235
Pionier-Bn. 235
235 Nachrichten-Abt.

11.Schützenbrigade (mot) – Obst. Angern
Infanterie Regt. 110
Infanterie Regt. 111
Maschinengewehr-Bataillon 13

Reserve
Panzer Abteilung zbV 40(-) – 1. and 2. Kompanie with 43 PzKpfw I/II
Maschinengewehr-Bataillon 4
Maschinengewehr-Bataillon 14
Artillerie-Abt 729 (motorized)
4.Kompanie/Fallschirmjäger Regiment 1 (Luftwaffe)
I Battailon/'General Göring' Rgt. (Luftwaffe)
Two battalions from SS 'Totenkopf' Regiment 6

Kreigsmarine

Fleet commander – Adm. Wilhelm Marschall
Aufklärungsgruppe (Covering/Scouting Group) – VAdm. Günther Lütjens
Gruppe 1 – Kdr. Bonte
Gruppe 2 – KsZ. Heye

Marine Gruppenkommando Ost (Naval Gruppe Command East) – Adm. Rolf Carls
Gruppe 5 – KAdm. Kummetz
Gruppe 7 – KzS. Kleikamp
Gruppe 8 – Klt. Schroeder
Gruppe 9 – Klt. Leissner

Marine Gruppenkommando West (Naval Gruppe Command West) – Adm. Alfred Saalwächter
Gruppe 3 – KAdm. Schmundt
Gruppe 4 – KsZ. Rieve
Gruppe 6 – Klt. Thoma
Gruppe 10 – Kdr. Ruge
Gruppe 11 – Klt. Berger

U-boot Gruppen
Ausfuhrstaffel
Tankerstaffel
Seetransportstaffeln

Luftwaffe

Fliegerkorps X – Gen.Lt. Hans Geisler
I/ZG.1
I/ZG.76
II/JG.77
I/StG.1
KG.4
I Gruppe
II Gruppe
III Gruppe
KG.26
I Gruppe
II Gruppe
KG.30
I Gruppe (-)
III Gruppe
Z.Staffel
KGr.100
1(Fern)/Aufklärungsgr.120
1(Fern)/Aufklärungsgr.122
2(Heeres)/Aufklärungsgr.10
KüstenFl.Gr.506
KGzbV.1
I Gruppe
II Gruppe
III Gruppe
IV Gruppe

Lufttransportsche Land –Obstlt. Carl von Gablenz
KGrzbV.101
KGrzbV.102
KGrzbV.103
KGrzbV.104
KGrzbV.105
KGrzbV.106
KGrzbV.107

Lufttransportsche See – Hpt. Förster
KGrzbV.108(See)

DANISH FORCES

Army

Jutland Division
2nd Infantry Regt.
3rd Infantry Regt.
6th Infantry Regt.
7th Infantry Regt.
Jutland Dragoon Regt.
3rd Field Arty Regt.
14th Anti-Aircraft Bn.
2nd Engineer Bn.

Zealand Division
Life Guards Regt.
1st Infantry Regt.
4th Infantry Regt.
5th Infantry Regt.
Guards Hussars Regt.
1st Field Arty Regt.
2nd Field Arty Regt.
13th Anti-Aircraft Bn.
1st Engineer Bn.

Army Air Corps
1.Eskadrille
2.Eskadrille
3.Eskadrille
5.Eskadrille

Navy

Two coastal defence ships
Six torpedo boats
Five patrol boats (ex-torpedo boats)
Ten submarines with one submarine tender
One minelayer and seven other minelaying vessels
Nine minesweepers

Naval Air Service
1.Luftflotille
2.Luftflotille

NORWEGIAN FORCES

Army

Commander – Gen.Maj. Kristian Låke (replaced by Obst. Otto Ruge, 11 April 1940)

1st Division – Gen.Maj. Carl J. Erichsen
1st Infantry Regt.
2nd Infantry Regt.
3rd Infantry Regt.
1st Dragoon Regt.
1st Artillery Regt.

2nd Division – Gen.Maj. Jacob Hvinden Haug
4th Infantry Regt.
5th Infantry Regt.
6th Infantry Regt.
1st Guards Bn.
2nd Dragoon Regt.
2nd Artillery Regt.

3rd Division – Gen.Maj. Einar Liljedahl
7th Infantry Regt.
8th Infantry Regt.
I Mountain Arty Bn.
3rd Cyclist Coy

4th Division – Gen.Maj. William Steffens
9th Infantry Regt.
10th Infantry Regt.
II Mountain Arty Bn.
4th Cyclist Coy

5th Division – Gen.Maj. Jacob Laurantzon
11th Infantry Regt.
12th Infantry Regt.
13th Infantry Regt.
3rd Artillery Regt.
3rd Dragoon Regt.
V Engineer Bn.

6th Division – Gen.Maj. Carl G. Fleischer
14th Infantry Regt.
15th Infantry Regt.
16th Infantry Regt.
III Mountain Arty Bn.
VI Engineer Bn.

Army Reserve
Anti-Aircraft Regt.
HQ Engineer Bn.

Army Air Service – Obst. Gulliksen
Jagervingen
Bombervingen
Speidevingen
Flygeskolen

Navy

Commander – KAdm. H. E. Diesen
1st Sea Defense District – KAdm. J. Smith-Johannsen
Oslofjord Flotilla
Kristiansand Flotilla

2nd Sea Defense District – KAdm. C. Tank-Nielsen
Bergen Flotilla
Trondheim Flotilla

3rd Sea Defense District – KAdm. L. Hagerup

Naval Air Service
1.Flyavdeling
2.Flyavdeling
3.Flyavdeling

ALLIED EXPEDITIONARY FORCES

Ground forces

Mauriceforce – Maj. Gen. Adrian Carton de Wiart, V.C.
British 146th (Territorial) Infantry Brigade – Brig. Charles G. Phillips
1st/4th Battalion, The Royal Lincolnshire Regiment
1st/4th Battalion, King's Own Yorkshire Light Infantry
1st/4th (Hallamshire) Battalion, York and Lancaster Regiment
French 5e Demi-Brigade Chasseurs Alpins – Commandant Brunelli
13e Bataillon Chasseurs Alpins
53e Bataillon Chasseurs Alpins
67e Bataillon Chasseurs Alpins

Sickleforce – Maj. Gen. Bernard C. T. Paget
British 15th Brigade – Brig. Herbert E. F. Smyth
1st Battalion, The Green Howards
1st Battalion, The King's Own Yorkshire Light Infantry
1st Battalion, The York and Lancaster Regiment
British 148th (Territorial) Infantry Brigade – Gen. Harold deR Morgan
1st/5th Battalion, The Royal Leicestershire Regiment
1st/8th Battalion, The Sherwood Foresters

Rupertforce – Maj. Gen. Pierse J. Mackesy
British 24th (Guards) Brigade – Brig, The Hon. William Fraser
1st Battalion, Scots Guards
1st Battalion, Irish Guards
2nd Battalion, South Wales Borderers
British 203rd Field Battery/51st Field Regiment, Royal Artillery
British 3rd King's Own Hussars (one troop; three Vickers Mk VIb light tanks)

French 1ère Division Légère de Chasseurs (-) – Gen. de brig. Antoine. E. Bèthouart
French 27e Demi-Brigade Chasseurs Alpins – Lt. Col. Valentini
6e Bataillon Chasseurs Alpins
12e Bataillon Chasseurs Alpins
14e Bataillon Chasseurs Alpins
French 13e Demi-Brigade de Légion Étrangère– Lt. Col. Magrin-Verneret
1er Bataillon
2e Bataillon
Polish Carpathian Podhale Brigade – Gen. Zygmunt Bohusz-Szyszko
1er Demi-Brigade – Col. Chlusevic
2e Demi-Brigade – Col. Kobylecki
French 2e Groupe Autonome d'Artillerie Coloniale
French 342e Compagnie Autonome de Chars de Combat

Rupertforce Support Troops
Royal Air Force component – Gp. Capt. M. Moore
No. 46 Squadron
No. 263 Squadron
British 6th Anti-Aircraft Brigade, RA – Brig. F. N. C. Rosseter
55th Light AA Regiment
56th Light AA Regiment (-)
51st Heavy AA Regiment
82nd Heavy AA Regiment (-)
British 1st, 2nd, 3rd, 4th, and 5th

Independent Companies (commandos)
Two light and one heavy independent AA Batteries, RA
Two field companies of Royal Engineers

Naval forces

Royal Navy Home Fleet
Commander – Admiral of the Fleet Sir Charles M. Forbes
2nd Battle Sqdn. – VAdm. L. E. Holland
Battle Cruiser Sqdn. – VAdm. W. J. Whitworth
Aircraft Carrier Sqdn. – VAdm. L. V. Wells
1st Cruiser Sqdn – VAdm. J. H. D. Cunningham
2nd Cruiser Sqdn – VAdm. G. F. Edward-Collins
18th Cruiser Sqdn – VAdm. G. Layton
2nd Destroyer Flotilla
3rd Destroyer Flotilla
4th Destroyer Flotilla
5th Destroyer Flotilla
6th Destroyer Flotilla
8th Destroyer Flotilla
10th Destroyer Flotilla
12th Destroyer Flotilla
2nd Submarine Flotilla
6th Submarine Flotilla

Reinforcing units

British
Aircraft carriers HMS *Ark Royal* and HMS *Glorious*
20th Cruiser Sqdn (AA Cruisers) – RAdm. J. G. P. Vivian
Anti-Aircraft Flotilla (AA Sloops) – Capt. A. L. Poland
1st Destroyer Flotilla
7th Destroyer Flotilla
20th Destroyer Flotilla
Fleet Air Arm
No. 800 NAS
No. 801 NAS
No. 803 NAS
No. 804 NAS
No. 810 NAS
No. 816 NAS
No. 818 NAS
No. 820 NAS
No. 821 NAS
No. 823 NAS

French
Naval Gruppe Z – Adm. E. H. H. M. Derrien

Polish
Three destroyers (attached to 1st Destroyer Flotilla)
Two submarines (attached to 2nd Submarine Flotilla)

Royal Air Force

Bomber Command
2 Group
No. 107 Sqn.
No. 110 Sqn.
3 Group
No. 9 Sqn.
No. 37 Sqn.
No. 38 Sqn.
No. 75 Sqn.
No. 99 Sqn.
No. 115 Sqn.
No. 149 Sqn.

Coastal Command
18 Group
No. 201 Sqn.
No. 204 Sqn.
No. 209 Sqn.
No. 220 Sqn.
No. 224 Sqn.
No. 233 Sqn.
No. 240 Sqn.
No. 254 Sqn.

Fighter Command
No. 29 Sqn.
No. 43 Sqn.
No. 111 Sqn.
No. 605 Sqn.

THE CAMPAIGN

The prerequisites for the success of the operation are surprise and rapid action ...
Executed with boldness, tenacity, and skill

Grossadmiral Erich Raeder, Instructions to Kriegsmarine Officers, 1 April 1940

OPENING MOVES

On the afternoon of 2 April, Adolf Hitler signed the operational order for *Weserübung*, setting into motion Grossadmiral Raeder's grand scheme. Four nights later Marine Gruppe 1, consisting of Kommodore Friedrich Bonte's ten modern destroyers, embarked 2,000 men of GJR 139 at Cuxhaven and moved into Schillig Roads to join the Kriegsmarine's two formidable battlecruisers, the *Gneisenau* and *Scharnhorst*. They were joined by Marine Gruppe 2, made up of Kapitän zur See Helmuth Heye's heavy cruiser *Admiral Hipper* and four destroyers, which carried 1,700 troops of GJR 138, loaded at Wesermünde. At midnight Central European Time[1] the largest German naval force of World War II steamed out of Schillig Roads under a dark moonless sky and headed north-north-west at 26 knots.

Recent RAF reconnaissance reports of large numbers of German warships gathering at North Sea ports led to the suspicion a major effort may be underway. Consequently, the next morning Coastal Command's No. 220 Squadron was out in strength, its Lockheed Hudson patrol bombers fanning out across the Skagerrak. One of them sighted a portion of the German force and radioed its position, strength (one cruiser and six destroyers) and course (northbound). The RAF organized an attack by 18 Bristol Blenheim light bombers (from Nos. 82 and 107 Squadrons) and these came roaring in just after noon. Braving fierce flak the attackers failed to gain a hit. The enemy fleet's slipping beneath the edges of a stormy weather front spoilt a follow-up raid by 24 Vickers Wellington medium bombers.

German *Gebirgsjäger* wait to board the heavy cruiser *Admiral Hipper* at Wesermünde on 6 April. Bound for Trondheim, these Bavarians would be fighting far from home. (Bundesarchiv Bild 101I-MW-5607-32)

The British destroyer *Glowworm* making smoke as it crosses the bow of *Admiral Hipper*. Doubling back to port the little warship was perfectly positioned to ram its adversary when *Admiral Hipper* ploughed ahead through the smoke. (Courtesy Imperial War Museum, London – FL1973)

1. Central European (Summer) Time is used throughout this narrative. It was one hour later than London or Greenwich Mean Time and times quoted in British references have been adjusted to CET in this account.

DEPLOYMENT OF NAVAL FORCES FOR THE INVASION OF NORWAY, 2000HRS, 8 APRIL 1940

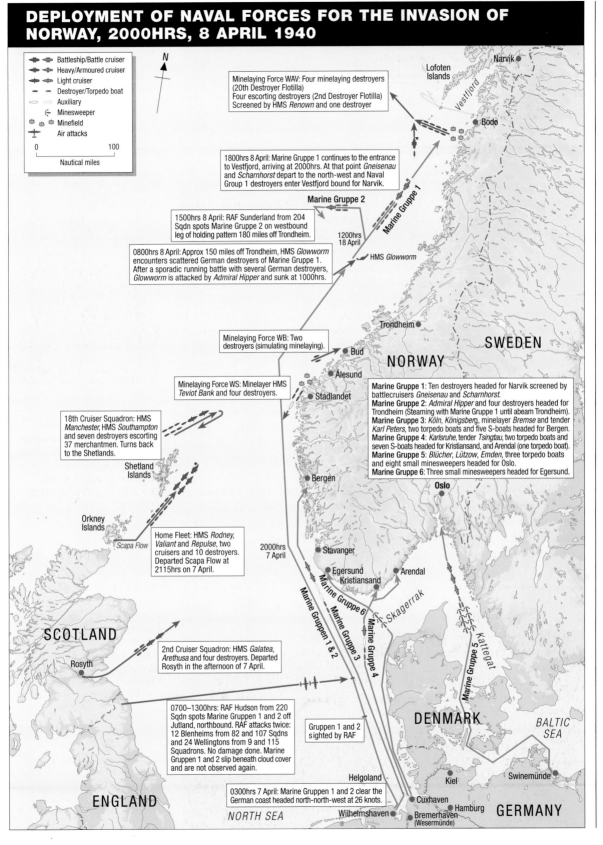

Legend:
- Battleship/Battle cruiser
- Heavy/Armoured cruiser
- Light cruiser
- Destroyer/Torpedo boat
- Auxiliary
- Minesweeper
- Minefield
- Air attacks

0   100
Nautical miles

N

Narvik

Lofoten Islands

Vestfjord

Bodø

Minelaying Force WAV: Four minelaying destroyers (20th Destroyer Flotilla)
Four escorting destroyers (2nd Destroyer Flotilla)
Screened by HMS *Renown* and one destroyer

1800hrs 8 April: Marine Gruppe 1 continues to the entrance to Vestfjord, arriving at 2000hrs. At that point *Gneisenau* and *Scharnhorst* depart to the north-west and Naval Group 1 destroyers enter Vestfjord bound for Narvik.

Marine Gruppe 2

Marine Gruppe 1

1500hrs 8 April: RAF Sunderland from 204 Sqdn spots Marine Gruppe 2 on westbound leg of holding pattern 180 miles off Trondheim.

1200hrs 18 April

HMS *Glowworm*

0800hrs 8 April: Approx 150 miles off Trondheim, HMS *Glowworm* encounters scattered German destroyers of Marine Gruppe 1. After a sporadic running battle with several German destroyers, *Glowworm* is attacked by *Admiral Hipper* and sunk at 1000hrs.

Trondheim

SWEDEN

Minelaying Force WB: Two destroyers (simulating minelaying).

Bud

NORWAY

Ålesund

Minelaying Force WS: Minelayer HMS *Teviot Bank* and four destroyers.

Stadlandet

18th Cruiser Squadron: HMS *Manchester*, HMS *Southampton* and seven destroyers escorting 37 merchantmen. Turns back to the Shetlands.

Marine Gruppe 1: Ten destroyers headed for Narvik screened by battlecruisers *Gneisenau* and *Scharnhorst*.
Marine Gruppe 2: *Admiral Hipper* and four destroyers headed for Trondheim (Steaming with Marine Gruppe 1 until abeam Trondheim).
Marine Gruppe 3: *Köln*, *Königsberg*, minelayer *Bremse* and tender *Karl Peters*, two torpedo boats and five S-boats headed for Bergen.
Marine Gruppe 4: *Karlsruhe*, tender *Tsingtau*, two torpedo boats and seven S-boats headed for Kristiansand, and Arendal (one torpedo boat).
Marine Gruppe 5: *Blücher*, *Lützow*, *Emden*, three torpedo boats and eight small minesweepers headed for Oslo.
Marine Gruppe 6: Three small minesweepers headed for Egersund.

Shetland Islands

Bergen

Orkney Islands

Oslo

Scapa Flow

Home Fleet: HMS *Rodney*, *Valiant* and *Repulse*, two cruisers and 10 destroyers. Departed Scapa Flow at 2115hrs on 7 April.

2000hrs 7 April

Stavanger

Egersund
Kristiansand

Arendal

Marine Gruppe 6

Marine Gruppe 5

Marine Gruppe 4

Marine Gruppe 3

Marine Gruppen 1 & 2

Skagerrak

Kattegat

SCOTLAND

2nd Cruiser Squadron: HMS *Galatea*, *Arethusa* and four destroyers. Departed Rosyth in the afternoon of 7 April.

Rosyth

0700–1300hrs: RAF Hudson from 220 Sqdn spots Marine Gruppen 1 and 2 off Jutland, northbound. RAF attacks twice: 12 Blenheims from 82 and 107 Sqdns and 24 Wellingtons from 9 and 115 Squadrons. No damage done. Marine Gruppen 1 and 2 slip beneath cloud cover and are not observed again.

Gruppen 1 and 2 sighted by RAF

DENMARK

BALTIC SEA

Helgoland

0300hrs 7 April: Marine Gruppen 1 and 2 clear the German coast headed north-north-west at 26 knots.

Kiel

Swinemünde

ENGLAND

NORTH SEA

Cuxhaven
Wilhelmshaven

Bremerhaven (Wesermünde)

Hamburg

GERMANY

Off their bows, at great range, were three groups of RN warships. The largest was headed for Vestfjord, the wide gateway to Narvik, with four mine-laden destroyers and their escort of four H-class destroyers (the 2nd Destroyer Flotilla under Captain Bernard A. W. Warburton-Lee) screened by the battlecruiser HMS *Renown* and four destroyers under Vice-Admiral William J. 'Jock' Whitworth. A smaller force, consisting of the 5,087-ton minelayer HMS *Teviot Bank* and four more destroyers, was sent to mine the Inner Leads near Ålesund. Vice-Admiral Whitworth's force had departed Scapa Flow on 5 April and at 0500hrs on 8 April began depositing their mines in Norwegian territorial waters. This was accompanied by a public announcement of the operation and delivery of an explanatory note to the Norwegian government.

As this drama unfolded, the RN's 18th Cruiser Division was escorting a convoy of merchant ships from the UK to Norway. Finally, on a sweep to round up enemy fishing trawlers in the North Sea were the cruiser HMS *Birmingham* and two more destroyers.

That fateful morning, HMS *Glowworm* from the Vestfjord group had missed the minelaying, having completed a vain search for a sailor swept overboard during the stormy night. At dawn the little ship was abeam Trondheim, racing north-east through heavy seas to rejoin VAdm. Whitworth's force when it ran into the German fleet. The destroyers of Marine Gruppe 1, scattered somewhat by the heavy weather, appeared occasionally and briefly out of the mist and spray and, turning away, quickly disappeared again, radioing their contact to VAdm. Lütjens. He ordered the *Admiral Hipper* to deal with the intruder and a short while later the heavy cruiser loomed out of the stormy mists, gunning for the little destroyer.

A one-sided battle ensued, Lieutenant-Commander G. Broadmead Roope attempted initially to flee and succeeded in sending a contact report before the mounting damage from *Admiral Hipper*'s crashing 20.3cm shells made it obvious that escape was impossible. Gallantly turning back against its powerful antagonist, *Glowworm* closed – taking repeated hits as she did so – for a torpedo attack. His ship severely damaged, burning and sinking, Lt. Cdr. Roope ordered one last, desperate and defiant attack, ramming the heavy cruiser in the starboard bow, sheering off 40m of armour belt and the starboard torpedo tubes. The *Glowworm* fell away, spent and dying, rolled over and blew up, taking all but 38 men with her. Lt. Cdr. Roope was posthumously awarded the Victoria Cross.

Though damaged, the *Admiral Hipper* was undeterred by the encounter and, after fishing the *Glowworm's* survivors from the tossing seas, KzS. Heye was ordered to maintain his position off Trondheim and wait for zero-hour the following morning. At 1500hrs, however, Heye's force was spotted by a Short Sunderland flying boat from No. 204 Squadron. The RAF snooper reported 'a battlecruiser, two cruisers and two destroyers' 290km off Trondheim, headed west. This news energized the Admiralty into action as it now appeared that the long-feared 'Atlantic breakout' of surface raiders was under way, which threatened to ravage the vital British convoys. The *Teviot Bank* was ordered home and the minelaying destroyers were ordered to rejoin VAdm. Whitworth's force. The latter rendezvoused with the destroyers at 1815hrs and headed off to the north-west to be better positioned to intercept the enemy on the morrow. In doing so they steamed into the teeth of a tempestuous Arctic gale.

Meanwhile Marine Gruppe 3, led by Konteradmiral Hubert Schmundt, departed Wilhemshaven shortly after midnight, bound for Bergen. At dawn Marine Gruppen 4 and 6 departed Cuxhaven for Kristiansand and Egersund respectively. The second largest task force, Marine Gruppe 5, comprising the brand new heavy cruiser *Blücher*, armoured cruiser *Lützow*, light cruiser *Emden*, three torpedo boats and eight motor minesweepers under Konteradmiral Oskar Kummetz, left for Oslo with 2,000 men at about the same time.

Also, late in the afternoon of the 8th, 24 He 111s from II/KG 26 raided Scapa Flow naval base in an attempt to damage the Home Fleet as it prepared to sail. Four Hawker Hurricanes from No. 111 Squadron intercepted them and destroyed four of the bombers. The raid was futile; the Home Fleet had already sailed.

However, Adm. Sir Charles M. Forbes was almost a day behind the events and was steering to cut off the phantom 'Atlantic breakout'. In fact, at 2000hrs on 8 April Marine Gruppe 1 arrived off the entrance to Vestfjord and Kdr. Bonte, sheered off and headed up the long, deep fjord with nine of his troop-laden destroyers; the *Erich Giese* had been separated in the rough seas and lagged behind the rest of the force. VAdm. Lütjens turned his two battlecruisers to the north-west to mark time while the landings took place, waiting for the appointed hour to rejoin the destroyers and begin the long voyage back to Germany.

In that very direction, enduring gale-force winds and high seas, was VAdm. Whitworth's force of HMS *Renown* and nine destroyers. During the night he had received orders from the Admiralty to 'concentrate on preventing any German force proceeding to Narvik'. It was some time before the gale let up to the point where he could bring his squadron about, but by morning the *Renown* was steaming south-east for Vestfjord with its destroyers in line astern.

At dawn, the *Renown's* lookouts suddenly spotted the dark silhouettes of two heavy warships steaming to the north-west. Immediately the captain of the *Renown*, Captain Charles E. B. Simeon, turned east to cut off the enemy warships. At a range of 17,500m HMS *Renown* hauled hard aport to parallel the enemy battlecruisers, swung its six 15in. guns to starboard and loosed a thunderous broadside.

The presence of the *Renown* was a total surprise to VAdm. Lütjens and his crews, nonetheless the *Gneisenau* and *Scharnhorst* went into action quickly and a heavy gun duel developed as the three capital ships plunged and ploughed ahead in the rough seas. The RN destroyers tried to keep up with their flagship and from well behind the battlecruiser contributed their own 4.7in. volleys, though they were pitifully out of range. However, the effect convinced Lütjens that he faced a much more formidable force than one capital ship and that, coupled with a shattering hit that knocked out the main fire-control system on the *Gneisenau*, prompted him to sheer away to the north-east and run headlong into the gale winds and towering rollers, accelerating to a speed of 28 knots.

Twice hit, though little damaged, *Renown* turned to chase, but could only make 20 knots in the rough seas and the enemy vessels disappeared into a snow squall. When they reappeared on the other side, the range was even greater and, even though the firing resumed, it was ineffective and short-lived. At 0715hrs the enemy ships disappeared completely. By then, the Nazis were two hours into their invasion of Denmark and Norway.

WESERTAG IN DENMARK

As Kriegsmarine vessels moved into their target harbours in Norway, at 0515hrs on Tuesday, 9 April 1940 – *Wesertag* ('Weser Day') – the German Army launched the briefest ground campaign on record. While the Danish Army had been forewarned of the invasion, it was prohibited from deploying or from preparing defensive positions because the

King Christian's capitulation ended Danish resistance before it began and German tanks rolled undeterred through Danish towns. (Bundesarchiv Bild 101I-754-051N-23)

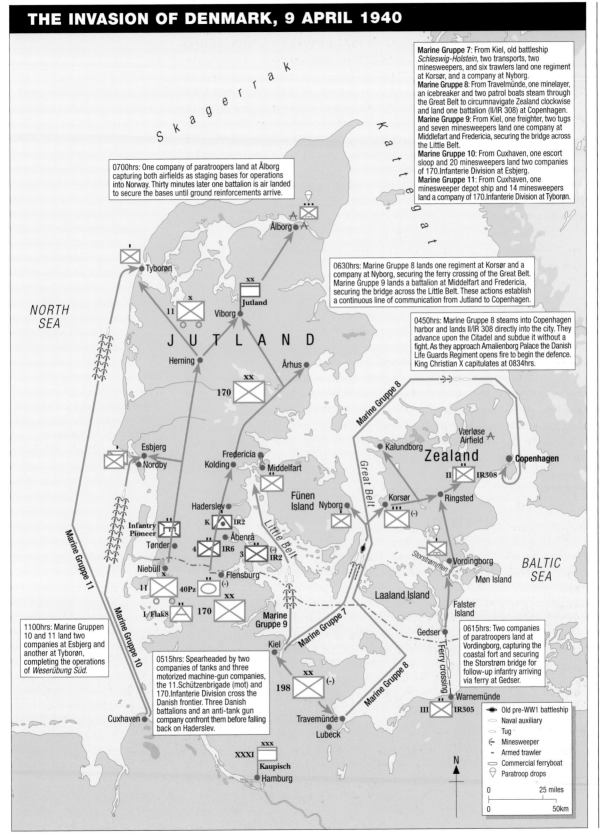

Marine Gruppe 7: From Kiel, old battleship *Schleswig-Holstein*, two transports, two minesweepers, and six trawlers land one regiment at Korsør, and a company at Nyborg.

Marine Gruppe 8: From Travelmünde, one minelayer, an icebreaker and two patrol boats steam through the Great Belt to circumnavigate Zealand clockwise and land one battalion (II/IR 308) at Copenhagen.

Marine Gruppe 9: From Kiel, one freighter, two tugs and seven minesweepers land one company at Middlefart and Fredericia, securing the bridge across the Little Belt.

Marine Gruppe 10: From Cuxhaven, one escort sloop and 20 minesweepers land two companies of 170.Infanterie Division at Esbjerg.

Marine Gruppe 11: From Cuxhaven, one minesweeper depot ship and 14 minesweepers land a company of 170.Infanterie Division at Tyborøn.

0700hrs: One company of paratroopers land at Ålborg capturing both airfields as staging bases for operations into Norway. Thirty minutes later one battalion is air landed to secure the bases until ground reinforcements arrive.

0630hrs: Marine Gruppe 8 lands one regiment at Korsør and a company at Nyborg, securing the ferry crossing of the Great Belt. Marine Gruppe 9 lands a battalion at Middlefart and Fredericia, securing the bridge across the Little Belt. These actions establish a continuous line of communication from Jutland to Copenhagen.

0450hrs: Marine Gruppe 8 steams into Copenhagen harbor and lands II/IR 308 directly into the city. They advance upon the Citadel and subdue it without a fight. As they approach Amalienborg Palace the Danish Life Guards Regiment opens fire to begin the defence. King Christian X capitulates at 0834hrs.

1100hrs: Marine Gruppen 10 and 11 land two companies at Esbjerg and another at Tyborøn, completing the operations of *Weserübung Süd*.

0515hrs: Spearheaded by two companies of tanks and three motorized machine-gun companies, the 11.Schützenbrigade (mot) and 170.Infanterie Division cross the Danish frontier. Three Danish battalions and an anti-tank gun company confront them before falling back on Haderslev.

0615hrs: Two companies of paratroopers land at Vordingborg, capturing the coastal fort and securing the Storstrøm bridge for follow-up infantry arriving via ferry at Gedser.

Skagerrak

Kattegat

NORTH SEA

Tyborøn

Ålborg

Viborg

Jutland

JUTLAND

Herning

Århus

170

Esbjerg

Nordby

Fredericia

Kolding

Middelfart

Fünen Island

Haderslev

Infantry Pioneer

Tønder

Åbenrå

Niebüll

Flensburg

40Pz

170

I/Flak8

Marine Gruppe 9

Kiel

198

Cuxhaven

Travemünde

Lubeck

XXXI Kaupisch

Hamburg

Marine Gruppe 11

Marine Gruppe 10

Marine Gruppe 8

Kalundborg

Værløse Airfield

Zealand

Copenhagen

II IR308

Korsør

Ringsted

Nyborg

Great Belt

Storstrømmen

Vordingborg

Møn Island

BALTIC SEA

Laaland Island

Falster Island

Gedser

Warnemünde

III IR305

Marine Gruppe 7

Marine Gruppe 8

Ferry crossing

K IR2

4 IR6

3 IR2

11

Little Belt

Old pre-WW1 battleship
Naval auxiliary
Tug
Minesweeper
Armed trawler
Commercial ferryboat
Paratroop drops

N

0 — 25 miles
0 — 50km

government did not want to provide the Germans with a provocation for their actions. The small, scattered units of frontier guards and elements of the Jutland Division were called out of their barracks at 0435hrs and began fighting delaying actions on the Jutland Peninsula.

At 0615hrs the airborne portion of the operation began with 96 paratroopers (from 4./FJR 1) descending from nine Ju 52/3m transports (from 8./KGzbV 1) to secure the bridge connecting Falster Island to Zealand and capture the nearby coastal fort at Vordingborg. This allowed a battalion (III/IR 305) of the 198.Infanterie Division disembarking at Gedser, at the southern tip of Falster Island, to race north to relieve the assault forces unloading at Copenhagen.

Meanwhile, two *Marine Gruppen* landed more troops from the 198.Infanterie Division to secure the connections between Jutland and Zealand. To capture the Jutland–Funen Bridge spanning the Little Belt 400 men were landed from Marine Gruppe 9. At the eastern end of Funen, the ferry route across the Great Belt was secured by another 1,990 men landed at Korsør and Nyborg by Marine Gruppe 7.

Copenhagen itself was taken by surprise: Marine Gruppe 8, the 2,430-ton auxiliary minelayer *Hansestadt Danzig*, escorted by the ice-breaker *Stettin* and a pair of patrol boats, steamed into the harbour at 0450hrs with their battle flags flying, illuminated by searchlights to be sure they would be seen. The guns of Fort Middelgrund watched in silence as the small flotilla sailed past, the fort's commandant so new to his post he had little idea what to do. Docking at a pier on the north end of the city, the ersatz troopship disgorged another battalion (II/IR 308) of the 198.Infanterie Division, which went ashore at 0518hrs. They moved quickly to the Citadel – the ancient fortress guarding the city and the headquarters of the Danish Army. After capturing the 70-man garrison without a shot being fired, the invaders marched on to Amalienborg Palace, the residence of the elderly King Christian X. There they finally met opposition, clashing with the King's Life Guard.

While the firefight at Amalienborg Palace was developing, a large formation of 28 He 111s from I/KG 4 roared over the city with an escort of Bf 110 Zerstörer from 3./ZG 1. The He 111s dropped no bombs as their mission was purely psychological: to demonstrate the strength of the Luftwaffe and thereby coerce the Danes into peaceful submission. The ploy worked as King Christian X was reluctant to see his beautiful Copenhagen become another devastated Warsaw and immediately ordered a ceasefire. By 0834hrs Denmark had surrendered to Hitler.

Meanwhile at Værløse airfield, north of the city, the opening act of *Weserübung* was played out. Anticipating the impending German invasion the Danish squadrons prepared for a widespread dispersal to airfields around the country. As the first Danish aircraft, a Fokker C.V-E, took off and climbed to a height of 50m the Bf 110s from 1./ZG 1 came roaring in with guns blazing. The hapless Fokker was shot down and the Zerstörer then strafed the airfield repeatedly, destroying seven Danish aircraft and damaging another 14.

As these events transpired, the two airfields at Ålborg in northern Denmark had been captured by a platoon of *Fallschirmjäger* (from 4./FJR 1) at 0700hrs. A stream of 53 Ju 52/3ms (I/KGzbV 1) delivered a battalion of infantry troops (III/IR 159) and, within an hour, the airfields were secured for use as staging bases against southern Norway.

LANDINGS IN NORWAY

As Denmark fell, the six other German *Marine Gruppen* boldly approached their respective objectives to land their embarked assault forces. However, the element of surprise – one of Grossadmiral Raeder's two essential prerequisites for success – had been lost the evening before when one of the German supply ships bound for Bergen, the 5,261-ton freighter *Rio de Janeiro*, was sunk by one of VAdm. Horton's submarines, which was on patrol off Lillesand. A Norwegian destroyer and fishing boats rescued the survivors only to learn, to their horror, that the Germans were headed for Bergen to 'protect' it from the British! Once the divisional commander at Kristiansand, Generalmajor Einar Liljedahl, was informed he immediately passed the alarm to the Norwegian army HQ and the government.

So now the conquest of Norway would depend on Raeder's remaining prerequisite, namely 'rapid action … executed with boldness, tenacity, and skill'.

Oslo

Undeterred by his midnight encounter with the Norwegian patrol boat *Pol III*, Konteradmiral Kummetz confidently led Marine Gruppe 5 up the narrowing Oslofjord as morning fog formed in the darkness. Once past the shore batteries on Raøy and Bolærne Islands, which bracketed the mouth of the fjord, he paused to land two companies to take the Norwegian fortifications from the rear and sent a third force to capture the naval base at Horton. The latter was met by fire from the 1,596-ton minelayer *Olav Tryggvason*'s 12cm guns, which sank one minesweeper and damaged the torpedo boat *Albatros*. The German force withdrew and put the assault troops ashore further down the fjord. Marching overland, they found the Horton naval base undefended from the landward side and captured it without firing a shot.

Surprise lost, Kummetz blithely continued up the narrowing fjord towards his ultimate objective of Oslo. By this time the sun was up and the

Insisting on sticking with the prescribed timetable despite the obvious loss of surprise, Konteradmiral Kummetz steamed the *Blücher* up Oslofjord to her death at the hands of Norwegian 28cm and 15cm guns, as well as shore-mounted torpedo tubes. (Norwegian Resistance Museum Neg. Nr. 4066)

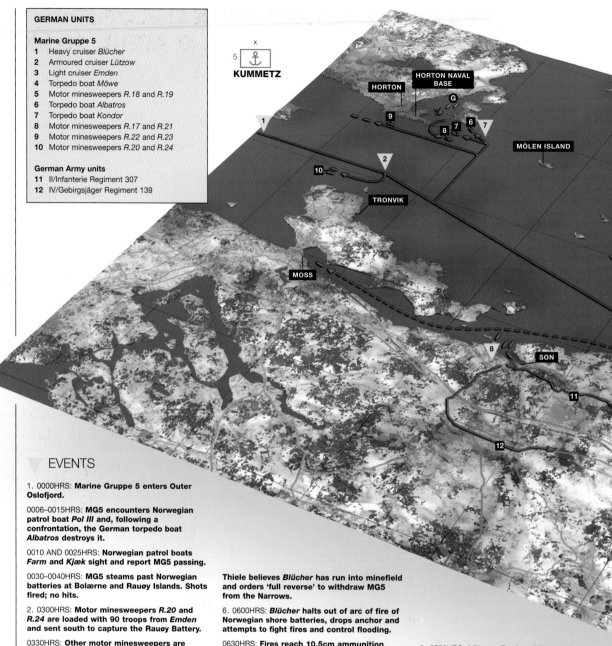

GERMAN UNITS

Marine Gruppe 5
1   Heavy cruiser *Blücher*
2   Armoured cruiser *Lützow*
3   Light cruiser *Emden*
4   Torpedo boat *Möwe*
5   Motor minesweepers *R.18* and *R.19*
6   Torpedo boat *Albatros*
7   Torpedo boat *Kondor*
8   Motor minesweepers *R.17* and *R.21*
9   Motor minesweepers *R.22* and *R.23*
10   Motor minesweepers *R.20* and *R.24*

German Army units
11   II/Infanterie Regiment 307
12   IV/Gebirgsjäger Regiment 139

KUMMETZ

HORTON

HORTON NAVAL BASE

MÖLEN ISLAND

TRONVIK

MOSS

SON

EVENTS

1. 0000HRS: **Marine Gruppe 5 enters Outer Oslofjord.**

0006–0015HRS: **MG5 encounters Norwegian patrol boat *Pol III* and, following a confrontation, the German torpedo boat *Albatros* destroys it.**

0010 AND 0025HRS: **Norwegian patrol boats *Farm* and *Kjæk* sight and report MG5 passing.**

0030–0040HRS: **MG5 steams past Norwegian batteries at Bolærne and Rauøy Islands. Shots fired; no hits.**

2. 0300HRS: **Motor minesweepers *R.20* and *R.24* are loaded with 90 troops from *Emden* and sent south to capture the Rauøy Battery.**

0330HRS: **Other motor minesweepers are loaded with troops from *Emden* to assault Horton Naval Base; TBs *Albatros* and *Kondor* are detached for fire support. MG5 resumes steaming towards Oslo.**

3. 0448HRS: **Filtvet Naval Station sights MG5 and reports its passing; Norwegian minesweeper *Otra* identifies and reports them as German.**

4. 0454HRS: **Passing Norwegian merchant ship *Sørland*, motor minesweepers *R.18* and *R.19* attack it with gunfire, setting it ablaze.**

5. 0521HRS: **Oscarsborg Fortress opens fire – first salvo hits *Blücher*. Husvik Battery opens fire – multiple hits on *Blücher*. Torpedo battery fires two – both hit *Blücher*.**

0530HRS: **Oscarsborg Fortress shifts fire to the *Lützow*, achieving repeated hits, knocking out the ship's forward 28cm turret. Kapitän**

Thiele believes *Blücher* has run into minefield and orders 'full reverse' to withdraw MG5 from the Narrows.

6. 0600HRS: **Blücher halts out of arc of fire of Norwegian shore batteries, drops anchor and attempts to fight fires and control flooding.**

0630HRS: **Fires reach 10.5cm ammunition magazine; explosion dooms ship.**

0700HRS: **Abandon ship ordered.**

0722HRS: **Blücher capsizes and sinks.**

7. 0535HRS: **Torpedo boats *Albatros* and *Kondor* escort motor minesweepers *R.17* and *R.21* to Horton Naval Base. The torpedo boats remain outside harbour while the motor minesweepers go in. Norwegian mine layer *Olaf Tryggvason* stationed in harbour entrance and, unsure of the minesweepers' identity, initially lets them pass, but realizing the error, opens fire on *R.17* as it approaches quay, setting it on fire. Depth charges explode sinking *R.17*. Norwegian minesweeper *Rauma* engages *R.21*, both ships hit and withdraw.**

0730HRS: **Albatros re-attempts to enter Horton Harbour and is driven off, damaged, by *Olaf Tryggvason***

8. 0700HRS: **Lützow, *Emden*, *Möwe* and two MMS land troops at Son and Moss. Mountain troops (IV/GJR 138) advance on Drøbak while infantry (II/IR 307) march toward Oslo.**

0800HRS: **Emden moves over to Horton, putting more troops ashore to take the naval base from landward side.**

0835HRS: **Horton Naval Base surrenders to German troops.**

9. 1417HRS: **Lützow returns to entrance to Drøbak Narrows and begins bombarding Oscarsborg Fortress with aft 28cm turret at a range of 16,000–17,000m.**

1900HRS: **Kondor and two small vessels land troops in Drøbak. They advance to Husvik Battery and capture it at 1915hrs.**

1925hrs: **Kondor approaches Oscarsborg with white flag to begin surrender negotiations.**

SEABORNE ASSAULTS IN OSLOFJORD, 9 APRIL 1940

Note: Gridlines are shown at intervals of 1km (1093yds)

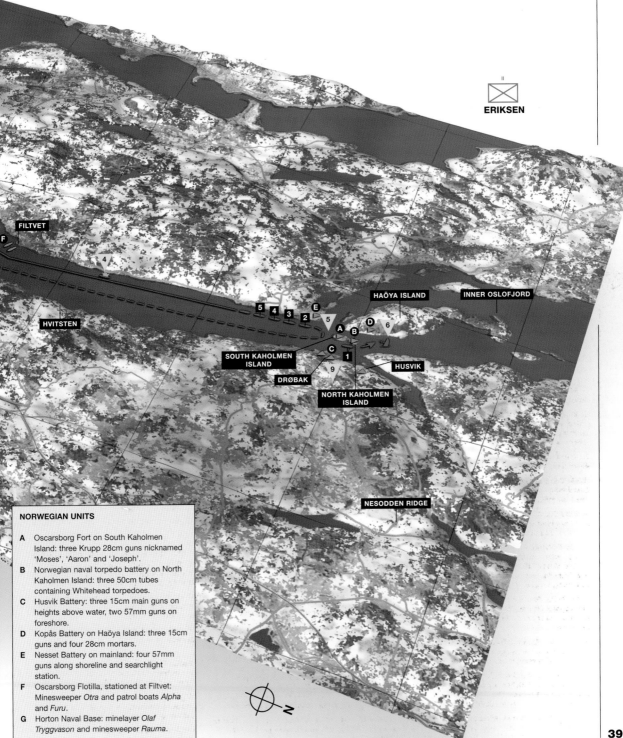

ERIKSEN

FILTVET

HVITSTEN

HAÖYA ISLAND

INNER OSLOFJORD

SOUTH KAHOLMEN ISLAND

DRØBAK

NORTH KAHOLMEN ISLAND

HUSVIK

NESODDEN RIDGE

N

NORWEGIAN UNITS

A Oscarsborg Fort on South Kaholmen Island: three Krupp 28cm guns nicknamed 'Moses', 'Aaron' and 'Joseph'.

B Norwegian naval torpedo battery on North Kaholmen Island: three 50cm tubes containing Whitehead torpedoes.

C Husvik Battery: three 15cm main guns on heights above water, two 57mm guns on foreshore.

D Kopås Battery on Haöya Island: three 15cm guns and four 28cm mortars.

E Nesset Battery on mainland: four 57mm guns along shoreline and searchlight station.

F Oscarsborg Flotilla, stationed at Filtvet: Minesweeper *Otra* and patrol boats *Alpha* and *Furu*.

G Horton Naval Base: minelayer *Olaf Tryggvason* and minesweeper *Rauma*.

mists had cleared and the German warships approached in full view the two fortresses bracketing the narrow throat of the fjord. On the east side of the narrows was the Husvik Battery of three 15cm guns. Across the 500m of water was the even more powerful Oscarsborg Fortress at Kaholmen with three 28cm guns and four torpedo tubes. As the Germans steamed brazenly between the two forts at point-blank range the Norwegians opened fire, the *Blücher* was hit from both sides with devastating effect. Amidships her floatplane hangar erupted with explosions while another hit wrecked the cruiser's steering gear. Then two torpedoes exploded violently against the port side of the ship, disabling the main engines and starting further fires. The ship coasted out of the arc of fire of the Norwegian guns and dropped anchor while the crew battled to save their ship.

Initially, the *Lützow* followed into the same jaws of destruction and three 28cm shells pounded the forward part of the ship. *Lützow* reversed course as quickly it could, leading the Marine Gruppe back to the south and safety. Meanwhile, north of the forts *Blücher* was racked by explosions in the 10.5cm ammunition magazine and began to roll over. Crowds of sailors and soldiers abandoned the stricken vessel and made it to the nearby shore, though 320 died when the cruiser finally capsized and sank.

The remaining German warships withdrew to put their troops (IV/GJR 139 and II/IR 307) on the east bank of the fjord at Son, some 32km short of their objective. They advanced to take the Drøbak Fortress from the rear, leaving it up to the Luftwaffe to take the Norwegian capital.

The air assault on Oslo consisted of three closely packed waves of aircraft. The first wave consisted of 28 He 111s (III/KG 26) to intimidate the Norwegian government into capitulation, but this force was delayed by weather. Led by Oberstleutnant Martin Drewes the second wave was made up of 29 Ju 52/3m transports (II/KGzbV 1) to deliver the paratroopers of 2./FJR 1 to Fornebu airfield, escorted by eight Bf 110C Zerstörer (1./ZG 76). Twenty minutes behind them were 53 more transports (KGrzbV 103) bringing in the infantrymen of II/IR 324.

To Obstlt. Drewes the fog and clouds, increasing as the German transports droned up the fjord, seemed to doom the operation and at 0720hrs he ordered the mission scrubbed and turned his formation back to land at Ålborg. Fliegerkorps X HQ also radioed the third wave to do the same but their commander, Hauptmann Richard Wagner, suspected this to be a Norwegian ruse and continued northwards.

Just after 0700hrs Kaptein Erling Munthe Dahl launched five Gloster Gladiators from Fornebu. They were led by Løytnant Rolf Thorbjørn Tradin and arrived over Steilene just in time to see the *Blücher* burning and dying. They soon spotted the lumbering Junkers transports emerging from the clouds and Lt. Tradin immediately ordered the attack, selecting one of the leading tri-motors as his target and shot it down.

As the Norwegian Gladiators started swooping down upon the lumbering transports the escorting Bf 110s, led by Oberleutnant Werner Hansen, engaged them. The Norwegian pilots spotted the approaching Zerstörer and, flying much more nimble biplanes, quickly turned the tables on them, shooting down two Bf 110s for the loss of one of their own. The Norwegian fighters were scattered by the fight and, as Oblt. Hansen continued to Fornebu to strafe two other Gladiators and the base's AA machine guns, the Jagervingen pilots were forced to land on various frozen lakes, with only one Gloster surviving the day.

Twenty minutes later the first KGrzbV 103 transports arrived through the fog and clouds to find the airfield in the clear. Hauptmann Wagner's Ju 52/3m attempted to land, but the Norwegian AA guns sprayed the slow transport, killing Wagner and forcing the pilot to climb away again.

Returning to strafe the machine-gun emplacements, one of the Bf 110s was hit, causing the right engine to catch fire. The pilot, Leutnant Helmut Lent, immediately landed straight ahead, surprising the defenders as his heavy fighter slid across the airfield and into a fence. At the same time Oblt. Hansen decided that the rest of his unit would have to do the same – his Bf 110s were almost out of fuel! The other Zerstörer landed behind Lent and, taxiing into the corners of the airfield, their rear gunners gave covering fire against the Norwegian machine-gun positions while the transports once again attempted to land, this time successfully.

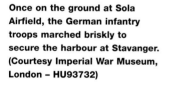

Once on the ground at Sola Airfield, the German infantry troops marched briskly to secure the harbour at Stavanger. (Courtesy Imperial War Museum, London – HU93732)

German infantry troops go ashore, protected by the powerful guns of the heavy cruiser *Admiral Hipper*. (Courtesy Imperial War Museum, London – HU93731)

The fierce, if brief, resistance by the Norwegian forts, small warships, Gladiator fighters and AA guns had given the nation's government just enough time to collect its wits and evacuate the capital. At 0830hrs, King Håkon VII, the Royal Family, the Cabinet, most members of the *Storting* (Norwegian Parliament) and a group of civil servants departed Oslo by train to Hamar, approximately 150km north of the capital.

Meanwhile, at Fornebu KGrzbV 103 brought in 350 men of II/IR 324 and the transports of II/KGzbV 1 returned to land two companies of paratroopers. While these troops disarmed the last Norwegian defenders and secured the airfield, 159 Ju 52/3ms of KGrzbV 101, 102 and 107 brought in more infantry, Luftwaffe ground service staffs and aviation fuel. Once the base was secure the German air attaché, Hauptmann Eberhard Spiller, organized six companies of infantry, led by the regimental band, for a march into Oslo.

By this time the *Storting* had heard the dreadful news from Trondheim, Bergen, Narvik and Copenhagen and evacuated even further to Elverum, closer to the Swedish frontier. Fortunately the on-scene commander of Norwegian army forces, Oberst Otto Ruge, had an infantry battalion (II Bn./5th Inf. Regt.) at hand and quickly established a blocking position between Hamar and Elverum.

Once Hpt. Spiller learned of the Norwegian government's location, he commandeered a collection of buses and trucks and, mounting two companies of FJR 1 on board, headed off to raid Elverum and capture King Håkon VII. With a paltry force and no element of surprise, the Germans were halted by the hasty Norwegian defences and were sent reeling back to Oslo with Hpt. Spiller mortally wounded.

Stavanger/Sola

The riskiest operation was at Stavanger and its nearby Sola Airfield, which were to be taken entirely by airborne assault. The forces involved consisted of one company of *Fallschirmjäger* (3./FJR 1), delivered by the 25 Ju 52/3ms of III/KGzbV 1, and supported by a squadron of He 111 bombers (8./KG 4) and followed by 104 Ju 52/3ms from KGrzbV 104 and 106 bringing in infantry troops to consolidate the invaders' hold on the strategic port and airbase.

The lead transports were to be escorted by eight Bf 110Cs (3./ZG 76) but they soon encountered thick fog and heavy clouds enshrouding the Skagerrak. Two of them collided in cloud and were lost, causing the flight leader to abort the mission. Nevertheless, two Bf 110s continued and were rewarded with clear skies over the target. They emerged from the murk and immediately began to shoot up the Norwegian ground defences as the first wave of Ju 52/3ms approached the drop zone.

On the ground, the Norwegian bomber squadron – three Ca 310s and six C.V-E biplanes – were just preparing for take off when the two Bf 110s and the eight He 111Ps arrived overhead. As the Zerstörer strafed, the Heinkels bombed, damaging one Caproni so badly it burst into flames. The remaining Norwegian bombers narrowly escaped as the first wave of Ju 52/3ms arrived and began disgorging their paratroopers. Although fired upon as they floated down, the 131 *Fallschirmjäger* assaulted the Norwegian defensive positions, capturing the airfield as the second wave of transports arrived.

The stream of Ju 52/3ms delivered two infantry battalions and the regimental staff of IR 193 without interference. The arriving infantry quickly organized themselves and marched down onto the port to secure it for the arrival of reinforcements, heavy weapons and supplies being delivered by the German merchant ships.

One of those ships never arrived. As the port fell to the invading Germans, the modern Norwegian destroyer *Æger* slipped out to sea. There it encountered the German merchantman *Roda* and sank it. Afterwards the *Æger* attempted to hide in Amøyfjord but was soon found and bombed by He 111s.

Kristiansand, Arendal and Egersund

Commanded by Kapitän zur See Friedrich Rieve, Marine Gruppe 4 arrived off Kristiansandfjord on schedule, but thick fog prevented it from entering the narrow and treacherous waters. At about 0623hrs the fog lifted enough to attempt entry but as the *Karlsruhe* approached, the Norwegian coastal fort on Odderøy Island opened up with its 21cm guns and drove the German warships away. KsZ. Rieve retired out of range and called for air support. The first raid proved ineffective but three hours later a follow-up attacks by 16 He 111s (2 and 3./KG 26) silenced the Norwegian batteries.

Rieve's assault troops landed and quickly stormed the fortifications, the dazed and demoralized defenders surrendering immediately. Soon afterwards the *Tsingtau* docked and began unloading the regimental staff of IR 310 plus one infantry battalion, which quickly secured the city and its environs.

Detached from Marine Gruppe 4, the torpedo boat *Greif* arrived off Arendal Harbour at 0850hrs bearing a 100-man bicycle-equipped troop from Aufklärungs-Abteilung 169 (the reconnaissance battalion of 69.Infanterie Division). These troops came ashore unopposed and captured the telephone cable station.

Similarly, at 0530hrs the three minesweepers of Marine Gruppe 6 arrived at the small port of Egersund with another 150 troops from Aufklärungs-Abteilung 169 on board. They too came ashore unopposed and captured the cable station, severing telecommunications with Britain just when the Norwegian government needed them most.

Bergen and Trondheim

Right on time Marine Gruppe 3 arrived off Bergen. There the cruisers transferred their contingents of 600 men each to the torpedo boats, S-boats and motor launches for the amphibious assaults on the coastal fortifications. After fending off attacks by two Norwegian Navy float-planes, KAdm. Schmundt sent his small craft to land the assault troops to capture the shore batteries at Kvarven and Sandviken and steamed his larger warships imperiously into the channel towards the port. Alerted, the old 21cm guns at Kvarven hit the *Königsberg* three times, causing significant damage, flooding and fires. The ship had to drop anchor to prevent drifting aground, and returned fire with its aft guns as damage-control parties fought the internal fires. As at other locations, the Luftwaffe was called in to deal with the defiant defenders. At 0706hrs a *Staffel* of He 111Ps (9./KG 4) arrived and quickly silenced the Norwegian forts.

The two Norwegian coastal defence ships *Norge* and *Eidsvold* were sent to protect the prize of the campaign: Narvik. Arriving on 7 April, they are seen resting peacefully at anchor the next day. (Norwegian Resistance Museum Neg. Nr. 12056)

Soon afterwards the *Bremse* arrived at the docks and landed Gen.Maj. Hermann Tittel, commander of the 69.Infanterie Division, and his staff plus two battalions of IR 159 who immediately began to secure their designated objectives in and around the second largest city in Norway.

Trondheim – the key to taking the entire length of the Norwegian coastline – proved to be the easiest of the main objectives for the Germans to secure. After sinking the *Glowworm* and marking time in the stormy seas, Marine Gruppe 2 arrived safely offshore their objective on time. At zero hour, KzS. Heye ordered his small force to steam into the fjord, declaring themselves to be British warships to get past the guns of the harbour defences. Realizing the ruse too late the Hysnes Battery opened fire as the warships sped past, the *Admiral Hipper* replying with two salvoes from her aft 20.3cm turrets. At 0530hrs the heavy cruiser anchored and the assault troops of GJR 138 were quickly put ashore. Trondheim surrendered without a fight.

Soon after noon 16 He 115s from 1. and 2./KüFlGr 506 arrived to begin searching for the British Home Fleet off the central Norwegian coast. For land-based aircraft an ice airstrip was hastily improvised and that afternoon six four-engined transports – five former Lufthansa FW 200s and the venerable Junkers G.38 from KGrzbV 105 – landed with the KüFlGr 506 ground crews and light flak batteries.

Narvik

Early in the morning of 9 April, nine of Kdr. Bonte's destroyers arrived safely at the entrance of Vestfjord and at 0300hrs continued into Ofotfjord at 27 knots. Ships peeled off for their pre-assigned tasks as they went. One was stationed as a picket while two others landed companies of *Gebirgsjäger* at Ramnes and Hamnes to secure the coastal batteries thought to be guarding the narrows.

Approaching Narvik through mist and patchy fog, three other destroyers sheered off to the north into Herjangsfjord to land I/GJR 139 at Bjerkvik. These troops moved immediately to the Elvegårdsmoen to

Once the Norwegian warships were eliminated the *Gebirgsjäger* could off-load their equipment from the crowded destroyers in relative safety. Here the *Hans Lüdemann* is unloaded at the Post Pier in Narvik harbour. (Courtesy Imperial War Museum, London – HU93722)

capture the Norwegian Army depot for the 6th Brigade, taking most of the defenders' heavy weapons without a shot being fired.

The flagship *Wilhelm Heidkamp* arrived off Narvik at 0415hrs with the fog thicker than ever and slowed to a stop confronted by the Norwegian coastal defence ship *Eidsvold*. The elderly 4,166-ton *Eidsvold* trained its 21cm guns at the impudent new German destroyer and fired a warning shot across its bow. Bonte immediately sent an officer by boat to the Norwegian warship to demand their surrender, but this was refused.

As the parlay went on, Korvettenkapitän Curt Rechel steered the *Bernd von Arnim* past the two warships, threading his vessel slowly amongst the throng of merchant shipping, headed for the Post Pier. The other Norwegian coastal battleship, the *Norge*, spotted the *von Arnim* and trained its guns on the intruder. Negotiations ended with a red warning flare from Bonte's representative and the *Heidkamp* fired four torpedoes. Two of them hit and the *Eidsvold* broke in two and sank, killing 262 Norwegian sailors.

As Rechel brought the *von Arnim* alongside the Post Pier, *Norge* opened fire but the salvo fell short. The *von Arnim* returned fire with all guns firing to starboard while the *Gebirgsjäger* crowded and crouched on the port side ready to leap to the pier once contact was made. Norwegian volleys flew wildly, sending rounds sailing into the town, as the *Norge* attempted to manoeuvre into a better position. But this also made it a better target and Rechel fired all his torpedoes. Two hit and the old warship burst into flames as it slowly rolled over and sank. Another 173 Norwegians died.

As this exchange of broadsides ripped the foggy air, the German mountain troops of II/GJR 139 leapt ashore and began spreading out to secure their objectives. Another company landed from the *Georg Thiele* and, finally, the *Heidkamp* docked and disembarked Gen.Lt. Dietl, his staff and more troops.

Dietl moved immediately to the local military headquarters where Oberst Konrad Sundlo, commander of the Narvik garrison, quickly surrendered the town. Two companies of Norwegian troops escaped, travelling up the ore railway towards the Swedish border, to establish a blocking position between the two.

DEPLOYMENT OF ROYAL NAVY FORCES TO COUNTER THE INVASION OF NORWAY, 9 APRIL 1940

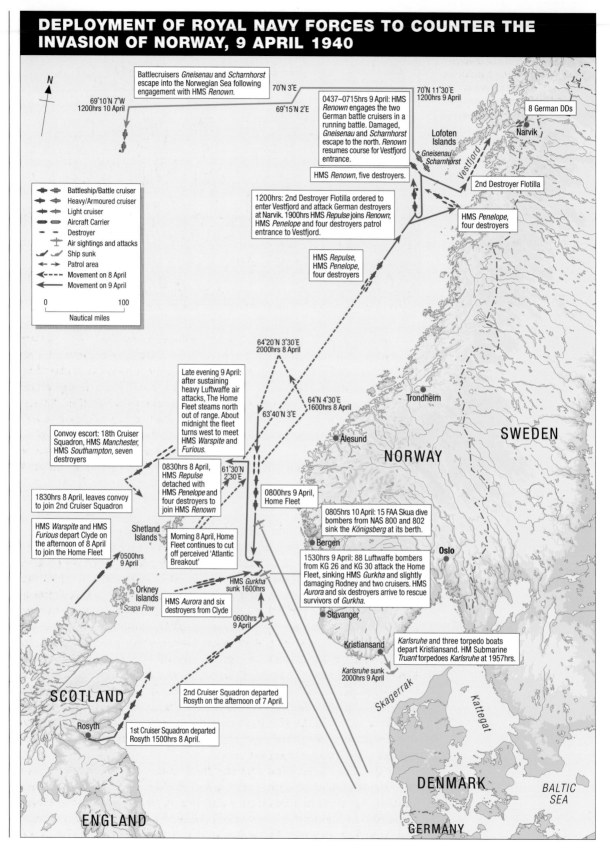

N

Battlecruisers *Gneisenau* and *Scharnhorst* escape into the Norwegian Sea following engagement with HMS *Renown*.

69°10'N 7°W
1200hrs 10 April

70°N 3°E

69°15'N 2°E

70°N 11°30'E
1200hrs 9 April

0437–0715hrs 9 April: HMS *Renown* engages the two German battle cruisers in a running battle. Damaged, *Gneisenau* and *Scharnhorst* escape to the north. *Renown* resumes course for Vestfjord entrance.

8 German DDs

Narvik

Lofoten Islands

Gneisenau
Scharnhorst

Vestfjord

HMS *Renown*, five destroyers.

2nd Destroyer Flotilla

1200hrs: 2nd Destroyer Flotilla ordered to enter Vestfjord and attack German destroyers at Narvik. 1900hrs HMS *Repulse* joins *Renown*, HMS *Penelope* and four destroyers patrol entrance to Vestfjord.

HMS *Penelope*, four destroyers

Legend

- Battleship/Battle cruiser
- Heavy/Armoured cruiser
- Light cruiser
- Aircraft Carrier
- - - Destroyer
- Air sightings and attacks
- Ship sunk
- ← → Patrol area
- ◄---- Movement on 8 April
- ◄── Movement on 9 April

0 _____ 100
Nautical miles

HMS *Repulse*, HMS *Penelope*, four destroyers

64°20'N 3°30'E
2000hrs 8 April

Late evening 9 April: after sustaining heavy Luftwaffe air attacks, The Home Fleet steams north out of range. About midnight the fleet turns west to meet HMS *Warspite* and *Furious*.

64°N 4°30'E
1600hrs 8 April

Trondheim

63°40'N 3°E

SWEDEN

Ålesund

NORWAY

Convoy escort: 18th Cruiser Squadron, HMS *Manchester*, HMS *Southampton*, seven destroyers

0830hrs 8 April, HMS *Repulse* detached with HMS *Penelope* and four destroyers to join HMS *Renown*

61°30'N 2°30'E

0800hrs 9 April, Home Fleet

1830hrs 8 April, leaves convoy to join 2nd Cruiser Squadron

Shetland Islands

Morning 8 April, Home Fleet continues to cut off perceived 'Atlantic Breakout'

0805hrs 10 April: 15 FAA Skua dive bombers from NAS 800 and 802 sink the *Königsberg* at its berth.

Bergen

HMS *Warspite* and HMS *Furious* depart Clyde on the afternoon of 8 April to join the Home Fleet

0500hrs 9 April

Orkney Islands

Scapa Flow

HMS *Gurkha* sunk 1600hrs

HMS *Aurora* and six destroyers from Clyde

0600hrs 9 April

Oslo

1530hrs 9 April: 88 Luftwaffe bombers from KG 26 and KG 30 attack the Home Fleet, sinking HMS *Gurkha* and slightly damaging Rodney and two cruisers. HMS *Aurora* and six destroyers arrive to rescue survivors of *Gurkha*.

Stavanger

SCOTLAND

Rosyth

2nd Cruiser Squadron departed Rosyth on the afternoon of 7 April.

Kristiansand

Karlsruhe and three torpedo boats depart Kristiansand. HM Submarine *Truant* torpedoes *Karlsruhe* at 1957hrs.

Karlsruhe sunk 2000hrs 9 April

1st Cruiser Squadron departed Rosyth 1500hrs 8 April.

Skagerrak

Kattegat

ENGLAND

DENMARK

BALTIC SEA

GERMANY

Waiting to refuel near-empty destroyers was the 11,766-ton *Jan Wellem*, a converted whaling ship that had arrived from Murmansk. Unfortunately the big ship lacked the fuel to completely refill the ten destroyers and had very slow pumps. The other crucial tanker, the 6,031-ton *Kattegat*, had almost made it to Narvik when it was challenged by the 266-ton Norwegian naval auxiliary *Nordkapp* and was scuttled in panic by its crew.

Despite his success, Bonte found himself unable to head for home. Even by leaving two empty destroyers for the seaward defence of Narvik it would be at least 36 hours before his force was ready for the run back to Germany.

THE ROYAL NAVY RESPONDS

Attempting to prevent the dreaded 'Atlantic breakout' Adm. Sir Charles Forbes steamed the Home Fleet out of Scapa Flow at 2115hrs on 7 April and headed north-east at high speed. About the same time Vice-Admiral Sir George F. Edward-Collins' 2nd Cruiser Squadron departed Rosyth and steered for an intercept point some 130km off Stavanger, planning to arrive there at 0600hrs the following morning and sweep northwards.

The next morning's chance encounter of the *Glowworm* with KzS. Heye's Marine Gruppe 2 was alarming news and Adm. Forbes pressed north-eastwards with renewed vigour to intercept the enemy squadron now about 290km ahead. When the RAF Sunderland reported Heye's squadron north of the Home Fleet and headed west, Sir Charles angled north-west on a projected interception course, taking the Home Fleet well away from the Norwegian coast.

By this time the Admiralty had totally abandoned Plan *R.4*. The troops and their equipment were disembarked at Rosyth and the 1st Cruiser Squadron put to sea immediately and headed north to join the Home Fleet. Also by this time a number of confusing and contradictory reports were flooding into the Admiralty. Most alarming was the British Naval

Attaché's report from Copenhagen that a battle/heavy cruiser, two cruisers and three destroyers (Marine Gruppe 5) had passed northwards through the Great Belt and into the Kattegat.

Admiral Forbes knew he had one German force north of him, last reported headed west, and another equally powerful force in the Kattegat perhaps coming out. He split his own force, sending HMS *Repulse*, one cruiser and four destroyers northwards to join VAdm. Whitworth's squadron and deal with the first enemy formation. Meanwhile, he turned south with his remaining warships to rendezvous with the 2nd Cruiser Squadron and deal with the second.

Farther south the 1st Cruiser Squadron joined the 18th Cruiser Squadron with Vice-Admiral Layton assuming command of the combined force. German intentions were finally revealed when, at 2355hrs, Adm. Forbes was at last told that the Polish submarine *Orzel* had sunk the transport *Rio de Janeiro* in the Skagerrak much earlier that day. Unfortunately, the three RN formations were too far off the Norwegian coast to intervene in any of the events of 9 April.

At first light, the Luftwaffe's *Küstenfliegergruppen* (coastal reconnaissance groups) swept the area between Bergen and the Orkneys with 28 He 115B twin-engine floatplanes, searching for British ships. They duly located and reported two major enemy surface groups: two battleships, six cruisers and a large destroyer screen north-west of Bergen (the Home Fleet) and nine cruisers and 11 destroyers to the port's west-south-west (the Cruiser Force).

With this knowledge, Fliegerkorps X mounted a large anti-shipping strike consisting of 41 He 111s from KG 26 and 47 Ju 88s from KG 30. The leading formation of Ju 88s found the cruiser force and dived heavily upon the British ships, sinking the destroyer *Gurkha* and damaging both the *Southampton* and *Galatea*. Further bomber formations found and attacked the Home Fleet, hitting the flagship with a bomb that failed to penetrate the *Rodney*'s thick deck armour. Three cruisers were damaged by near misses. The RN ships' AA fire was effective, bringing down four

Ju 88s with the loss of all crews. While, overall, damage was slight Adm. Forbes elected to retire out of range of Fliegerkorps X.

Meanwhile at Narvik, Kdr. Bonte's force settled into the routine of refuelling as VAdm. Whitworth's force arrived off the entrance to Vestfjord. At midday the Admiralty reported: 'Press states one German ship has arrived Narvik and landed a small force. [And to Capt. Warburton-Lee, senior officer of RN destroyers present:] Proceed Narvik and sink or capture enemy ship.' On this faulty intelligence, that afternoon Capt. Warburton-Lee headed up the long passage to Narvik with his 2nd Destroyer Flotilla, increased to five ships by the arrival of HMS *Hostile*. He planned to attack at dawn, when the tide was in and surprise was possible.

At Narvik, Bonte spread his flotilla out among the adjacent feeder fjords and posted U-boats in the Vestfjord to warn of an approaching enemy. However, the passing snow squalls concealed the British destroyers' approach. At 0510hrs, as the snowfall abated and dawn began to break, Warburton-Lee's flagship manoeuvred quietly in the snowy, early morning gloom, achieving a perfect firing position on the three visible German destroyers.

At 0530hrs HMS *Hardy* unleashed its torpedoes and crashing explosions shattered the early morning silence. The German flagship, *Wilhelm Heidkamp*, was hit in its aft magazine and blew up, killing 81 sailors, including Kdr. Bonte. The *Diether von Roeder* was hit repeatedly by 4.7in. shells, which caused heavy damage and started numerous fires.

As the *Hardy* pulled away, *Hunter* and *Havock* moved into position to continue the barrage and the carnage. *Hunter* hit *Anton Schmitt* with two torpedoes; it broke in half and sank at once, killing 50. Reacting slowly the *Hans Lüdemann* and *Hermann Künne* – both refuelling from the tanker – slipped their cables and went into action. Totally confused, their fire was wildly inaccurate and they took repeated hits.

After a second attack accomplished little due to the mist thickening and obscuring the possible targets, Warburton-Lee turned his destroyers around and headed back towards the entrance to Ofotfjord at a speed of 15 knots. As the five British destroyers headed down the narrow

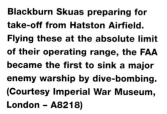

Blackburn Skuas preparing for take-off from Hatston Airfield. Flying these at the absolute limit of their operating range, the FAA became the first to sink a major enemy warship by dive-bombing. (Courtesy Imperial War Museum, London – A8218)

THE DESTROYER BATTLE IN NARVIK HARBOUR, 10 APRIL 1940 (pages 50–51)

A few moments after dawn – at high tide and through intermittent light snow squalls – Captain Bernard A. W. Warburton-Lee steered his flagship, HMS *Hardy* (1), into Narvik harbour and slowly turned about to come broadside to the two German destroyers visible in the hazy morning twilight. Beyond the screen of merchant shipping crowding the harbour the enemy flagship, *Wilhelm Heidkamp* (2), could be plainly seen and Flotilla Torpedo Officer Lieutenant G. R. Heppel gasped, 'There's a torpedo target such as I've never seen in my life!' Captain Warburton-Lee responded with 'Well get on with it then.' After a touch of engine revolutions to bring the *Hardy* about into a perfect beam firing solution, Heppel unleashed three torpedoes from the forward tubes;

all ran hot, straight and true, with the centre 'fish' hitting the aft quarter of its target. Immediately Warburton-Lee ordered revolutions for 20 knots and turned farther port towards the harbour entrance. As the *Hardy* moved and the view through the screen of merchant shipping changed, additional German destroyers were revealed. Heppel immediately ordered the aft tubes (3) swung to starboard and the crew tried frantically – against the slippery footing of the icy deck and the increased resistance of the cold mounting pivot – to move the 10-ton weapon into firing position. Meanwhile, in the distance, the morning calm was shattered by the explosion of the *Heidkamp*'s aft ammunition magazine, killing Kdr. Bonte and 80 other German sailors and throwing the ship's aft three 12.7cm gun turrets into the air. The destruction of the German destroyer squadron at Narvik had begun.

After being hit by three SAP500 bombs and having her hull split by a near miss, the *Königsberg* lingered before sinking. Bomb hits knocked out electrical power making firefighting and flood control impossible. (Norwegian Resistance Museum Neg. Nr. 6102)

waterway, suddenly from starboard three German destroyers emerged from Herjangsfjord in line astern. Immediately a running gun battle erupted, with neither side scoring any hits, and Frigattenkapitän Erich Bey quickly broke off the chase on account of a lack of fuel.

However, some 16km down Ofotfjord two more German destroyers – *Georg Thiele* and *Bernd von Arnim* – suddenly loomed out of Ballangenfjord, crossing the *Hardy's* bow firing full broadsides. German 12.7cm shells pounded the British flagship, killing or wounding everyone on the bridge, including Warburton-Lee. The shattered and burning destroyer swerved out of line and beached herself on the shore.

Next, *Hunter* drew the enemy's fire and, ablaze, out of control and losing headway, she slewed sideways in front of *Hotspur* which, heavily hit, ploughed into the flank of her mortally wounded sister. *Havock* and *Hostile* swerved around the two locked destroyers and passed the *Thiele* and *von Arnim* close aboard, guns roaring at each other at point-blank range. Finally, the battered *Hotspur* extricated herself from the clutches of the blazing and sinking *Hunter* and escaped after the other two.

Safely returning to the entrance of Vestfjord, the three British destroyers encountered the German supply ship *Rauenfels*. HMS *Havock* put a round into it, starting a fire, and the crew quickly abandoned ship. Two salvoes later the freighter erupted with a tremendous blast. In the destruction of the *Rauenfels* went almost all Gen.Lt. Dietl's artillery: GAR 112's battery of 150mm guns, three batteries of 88mm and 37mm flak guns, and all their ammunition.

For the British, Capt. Warburton-Lee's bold initiative and resolute determination had turned the tables in the far north of Norway, but at a terrible cost: 147 men killed and two destroyers sunk, a third badly damaged. For his courageous leadership and ultimate sacrifice, Capt. B. A. W. Warburton-Lee was posthumously awarded the Victoria Cross.

While the inability of the Home Fleet to intervene in the desperate situation of 9 April was a great disappointment, the nation's Senior Service soon scored several major victories, exacting from the invaders a high price for their audacious enterprise.

The first was provided by the RN's aviation branch, the Fleet Air Arm. At 0515hrs on 10 April, 16 Blackburn Skua two-seat fighter/dive-bombers of Nos. 800 and 803 NAS departed Hatston Airfield headed for Bergen, the very limit of the aircraft's operational range. Led by Lieutenant William P. Lucy, RN, their target was the damaged light cruiser *Königsberg*.

Two hours later the formation appeared over Bergen Harbour and Lt. Lucy positioned his formation up-sun for the attack. Attacking the immobile vessel the Skuas delivered their 500lb semi-armour-piercing bombs from 60-degree dives. With no opposition and delivered in clear, still air, two bombs hit the ship amidships while another struck the forecastle and a near miss opened a large hole in the cruiser's side. *Königsberg* languished – ablaze and settling by the bow – for two hours before an internal explosion caused it to sink.

Fifteen Skuas made it back to Hatston with only two of them damaged by flak. They landed on fumes, one pilot logging a four hour 30 minute flight in an aircraft that had an official endurance of four hours and 20 minutes!

Meanwhile, the German warships were returning individually to the protection of their Kriegsmarine bases. To catch them en route, VAdm.

Horton spread a cordon of 18 submarines across the Kattegat and Skagerrak. On the evening of 9 April the light cruiser *Karlsruhe*, steaming back from Kristiansand with three torpedo boats (Marine Gruppe 4), was torpedoed and sunk by HMS *Truant*.

Similarly, about midnight the following night, the armoured cruiser *Lützow* was torpedoed in the stern by HMS *Spearfish*. In this case the German warship did not sink but, after being towed to Kiel, was out of the war for 12 months. Additionally, during the next week British submarines also sank four freighters, two transports and two tankers. Two submarines were lost in these efforts: HMS *Thistle* to the *U.4* while trying to sneak into Stavanger harbour on the night of 9 April, and HMS *Sterlet* after sinking the minelayer/gunnery training ship *Brummer*, which was escorting a convoy through the Kattegat on 15 April.

Meanwhile VAdm. Lütjens steamed the *Gneisenau* and *Scharnhorst* – both battlecruisers having been damaged by the heavy seas while fleeing from *Renown* – well to the west, headed generally southwards in a broad zigzag pattern. At 0930hrs on 12 April he was joined by *Admiral Hipper* for the final dash home.

Finally, after a frustrating three days and nights of wild chases, shifting priorities and enemy air attacks Adm. Sir Charles Forbes reorganized his fleet. He sent nine light cruisers and a host of fuel-starved destroyers to Scapa Flow for refuelling and headed north to join VAdm. Whitworth off Narvik, which at this point became the sole objective of the British response.

He had been joined on 10 April by the aircraft carrier HMS *Furious* embarking 18 Fairey Swordfish TSR biplanes (816 and 818 NAS) and the 36,450-ton battleship HMS *Warspite*. The following day *Furious* delivered the first-ever carrier-launched air attack, all 18 Swordfish attacking two German destroyers with torpedoes in Trondheimfjord. No hits were scored because the weapons grounded in the shallows of the enemy anchorage.

At Narvik Fgtkpt. Bey began planning for a defence against the RN forces he knew were gathering offshore. One ship, the *Diether von Roeder*, which was immobilized from the first battle, was moored to the Post Pier for harbour defence. A second, the *Erich Koellner*, had run aground in Narvik harbour and was irreparably damaged, so she was positioned as a floating battery near the entrance to Ofotfjord. The other six he planned on deploying into the side fjords upon receiving word of the approaching enemy.

The German destroyer *Georg Thiele* fought valiantly and, once all rounds were expended, Korvettenkäpitan Max-Eckart Wolff ran her aground to save the surviving crewmen. (Courtesy Imperial War Museum, London – A24)

At 0830hrs the next morning VAdm. Whitworth headed up Vestfjord with *Warspite* and nine destroyers. Warned at 1010hrs Fgtkpt. Bey immediately ordered steam raised and his ships deployed, but it was too late to set up the intended trap.

Fortunately, Captain Victor A. C. Crutchely, VC and DSC, sent the *Warspite*'s catapult-launched floatplane ahead to scout the shoreline and side fjords and it soon reported the location of the *Koellner*. Looking into Herjangsfjord the pilot, Petty Officer (Airman) F. C. 'Ben' Rice, sighted the *U.64* on the surface recharging its batteries. Attacking from 300m, Rice dropped two 100lb anti-submarine bombs, one of which was a direct hit. The U-boat sank in 30 seconds with the loss of 12 crewmen.

Approaching the *Koellner*, three British Tribal-class destroyers engaged with full broadsides and in ten minutes battered the luckless warship into a hulk. A few minutes later the *Warspite* steamed by and performed the *coup de grâce* with six salvoes from its 15in. guns.

As the British entered Ofotfjord four German destroyers emerged from Narvik Harbour and made one attack before the Tribals drove them back. In an hour of hard fighting the Germans were crowded into the end of the fjord, running out of ammunition as well as manoeuvring room.

At the harbour entrance the *Erich Geise* made a stand, hitting HMS *Punjabi* six times and driving her away with 14 dead and 28 wounded. *Geise* was in turn blasted into a drifting, burning wreck by *Bedouin* and *Warspite*. The entrance open, HMS *Cossack* then steamed in to eliminate the immobile *von Roeder*. Manoeuvring broadside to the enemy at 1,800m, she was pummelled by an accurate, rapid-fire barrage from the German's two guns. Crippled by seven hits in two minutes, *Cossack* drifted aground at Ankenes with nine dead and 21 wounded. *Von Roeder* was then abandoned and destroyed.

Künne – undamaged but out of ammunition – beached herself in Herjangsfjord and was abandoned and blown up. Four others fled into Rombaksfjord, three of them continuing to the very end of the fjord where they were beached, with the crews escaping onto the rocky shore. The *Georg Thiele* made a stand and, though hit repeatedly by her pursuers, blew the bow off HMS *Eskimo* with her last torpedo. Once the

German captain learned that the last round had been fired he ordered 'full ahead' and ran his ship hard aground. The crew, minus 14 dead, escaped ashore to join their comrades and the now isolated German mountain troops.

The following day VAdm. Whitworth departed Ofotfjord, informing the Admiralty as he left that the Germans ashore appeared stunned and disorganized. He recommended a landing force be sent to occupy the town without delay.

THE ALLIES ARRIVE

On the morning of 10 April, with the consolidation of the immediate Oslofjord area complete, Gen.Maj. Erwin Engelbrecht began to move columns of his 163.Infanterie Division out of the city to overrun the scattered, slowly reacting units of the Norwegian 1st Division.

To begin the offensive drive northwards into central Norway, Gen.Lt. Richard Pellengahr's 196.Infanterie Division arrived on 11 April and mounted the drive towards Trondheim. The narrow valleys, deep snows and sparse roads leading northwards from Oslo limited the advance to two independent fronts. One *Kampfgruppe* (a 'battlegroup' formed around IR 324 and 345), under Pellengahr himself, began pushing up the Gudbrandsdal towards Hamar while another, formed around IR 340 under Oberst Hermann Fischer, side-stepped eastwards and advanced up the Østerdal to Elverum.

That same day the elderly and lethargic Gen. Låke was removed from command of the Norwegian Army and appointed in his place was Oberst Otto Ruge, who was immediately promoted to *Generalmajor*. Travelling 160km to the army's HQ at Rena that day he found he only had effective control over the 2nd Division.

Mobilized under great difficulty, the 2nd Division, under Gen.Maj. Jacob Hvinden-Haug, was able to field only two infantry battalions, a regiment of dragoons and three batteries of 75mm guns, and initially held

German forces were well equipped with heavy artillery, such as this leFH 18 105mm howitzer of AR 233 seen heading north out of Oslo for the front. (Courtesy Imperial War Museum, London – HU93720)

Replacing a company of light tanks lost when the freighter *Antares* was sunk by a British submarine, three experimental NbFz B 'land battleships' were unloaded with great publicity on the Oslo docks. (Bundesarchiv Bild 183-L03744)

Soldiers of the British 146th Brigade crowd the deck of SS *Oronsay* as Mauriceforce steams into Namsos Harbour. HMS *Fury* provides close escort. (Courtesy Imperial War Museum, London – N42)

the line between Hurdal and Eidsvoll. However, the units were handicapped by poor communications, consequently giving up this excellent defensive position following a few probes by German reconnaissance and mountain troops.

Well behind the lines, the Norwegians' one bright spot was the defeat and capture of an entire company of German paratroopers at Dombås, where the rail line up the Gudbrandsdal splits off to Trondheim. On the evening of 14 April, in terrible weather, 162 paratroopers (1./FJR 1 under Oberleutnant Herbert Schmidt) jumped into an enemy stronghold. The Norwegians had heavily defended the strategic railway intersection and took most of the company prisoner. The remnant, some 34 men, held out for four days and surrendered only when all food and ammunition was exhausted.

Despite this setback, by the evening of 19 April the Norwegian withdrawals had allowed Pellengahr to take both Hamar and Elverum in his two-pronged advance. He was aided by the arrival at the front of the

THE GERMAN CAPTURE OF SOUTHERN AND CENTRAL NORWAY, 12 APRIL–3 MAY 1940

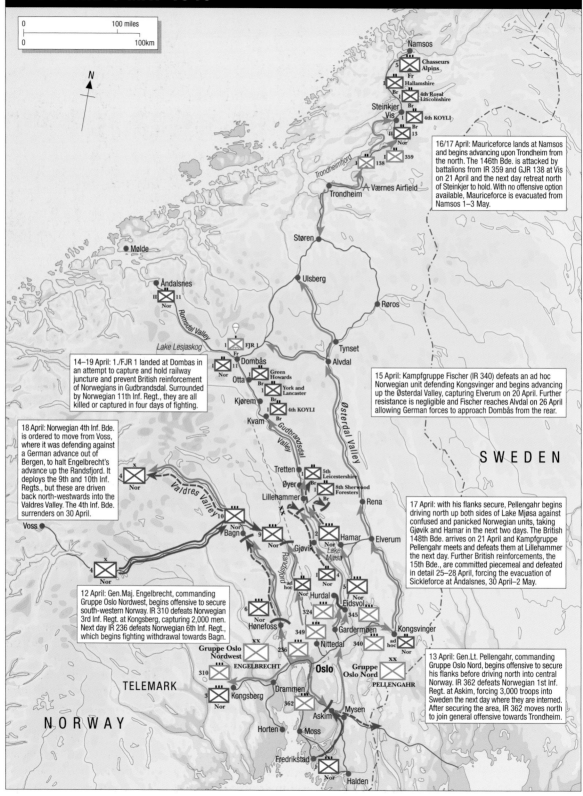

16/17 April: Mauriceforce lands at Namsos and begins advancing upon Trondheim from the north. The 146th Bde. is attacked by battalions from IR 359 and GJR 138 at Vis on 21 April and the next day retreat north of Steinkjer to hold. With no offensive option available, Mauriceforce is evacuated from Namsos 1–3 May.

14–19 April: 1./FJR 1 landed at Dombas in an attempt to capture and hold railway juncture and prevent British reinforcement of Norwegians in Gudbrandsdal. Surrounded by Norwegian 11th Inf. Regt., they are all killed or captured in four days of fighting.

15 April: Kampfgruppe Fischer (IR 340) defeats an ad hoc Norwegian unit defending Kongsvinger and begins advancing up the Østerdal Valley, capturing Elverum on 20 April. Further resistance is negligible and Fischer reaches Alvdal on 26 April allowing German forces to approach Dombås from the rear.

18 April: Norwegian 4th Inf. Bde. is ordered to move from Voss, where it was defending against a German advance out of Bergen, to halt Engelbrecht's advance up the Randsfjord. It deploys the 9th and 10th Inf. Regts., but these are driven back north-westwards into the Valdres Valley. The 4th Inf. Bde. surrenders on 30 April.

17 April: with his flanks secure, Pellengahr begins driving north up both sides of Lake Mjøsa against confused and panicked Norwegian units, taking Gjøvik and Hamar in the next two days. The British 148th Bde. arrives on 21 April and Kampfgruppe Pellengahr meets and defeats them at Lillehammer the next day. Further British reinforcements, the 15th Bde., are committed piecemeal and defeated in detail 25–28 April, forcing the evacuation of Sickleforce at Åndalsnes, 30 April–2 May.

12 April: Gen.Maj. Engelbrecht, commanding Gruppe Oslo Nordwest, begins offensive to secure south-western Norway. IR 310 defeats Norwegian 3rd Inf. Regt. at Kongsberg, capturing 2,000 men. Next day IR 236 defeats Norwegian 6th Inf. Regt., which begins fighting withdrawal towards Bagn.

13 April: Gen.Lt. Pellengahr, commanding Gruppe Oslo Nord, begins offensive to secure his flanks before driving north into central Norway. IR 362 defeats Norwegian 1st Inf. Regt. at Askim, forcing 3,000 troops into Sweden the next day where they are interned. After securing the area, IR 362 moves north to join general offensive towards Trondheim.

SWEDEN

TELEMARK

NORWAY

In contrast to the well-equipped Germans, British forces had to rely on local Norwegian generosity; Mr Sellæg's horses are seen here towing a 40mm Bofors into position at Hæknes. (Courtesy Imperial War Museum, London – N77)

light tanks of 1.Kompanie, Panzer Abteilung 40, which had been shipped from Denmark. On 17 April three NbFz B heavy tanks of Panzerzug Horstmann were unloaded on the Oslo docks and paraded through the city to join Pellengahr's battlegroups.

Also at Oslo, Generalmajor Kurt Woytasch's 181.Infanterie Division, was unloaded and organized for employment. Elements of the division were airlifted into Trondheim from 18 April, arriving in 600 transport sorties in the first week. The airlift was supplemented by one merchantman running the British blockade and two submarines reconfigured as undersea transports. By 21 April sufficient infantry battalions were at Trondheim to allow Obst. Weiss' *Gebirgsjäger* to begin driving northwards to relieve Dietl's beleaguered regiment.

Recognizing that his only real option was to delay the German advance towards Trondheim long enough for Allied forces to arrive, Gen.Maj. Ruge petitioned the British liaison officer to reinforce him as soon as possible.

The forces immediately available for such an action were on their way to Narvik: two British brigades, the 24th (Guards) Brigade and the 146th (Territorial) Brigade, aboard a convoy of five large troopships. In London the euphoria of VAdm. Whitworth's victory over the German destroyers at Narvik began to muddle the thinking of the War Cabinet. Believing – based on Whitworth's last message – that Narvik could be captured by the landing of a single brigade directly into the town, on 14 April they ordered Lord Cork and Orrery to do so and diverted the 146th Brigade to Namsos to re-take Trondheim from the north.

The 24th Brigade, continuing to Narvik, became the basis for Rupertforce, named by Churchill after the dashing Cavalier commander. And the 146th Brigade became the basis for Mauriceforce, after the bold Prince of Nassau who drove the Spanish out of the Netherlands.

But by splitting the force originally intended for Narvik, the British made a mess of an already slipshod operation. When the two transports containing the 146th Bde. turned south for Namsos they had no artillery or AA guns, or even their brigade commander, Brigadier C. G. Phillips.

Alerted that the transports were inbound, Captain Frank H. Pegram, commanding a small cruiser force searching for German shipping in the Leads north of Stadtlandet, put a 350-man naval landing force ashore at Namsos on 14 April and the 146th Bde. unloaded in relative security over the next two days. The operational commander, Major-General Adrian Carton de Wiart, VC and DSO, a hero of World War I and commander of the 61st Division, arrived by RAF Sunderland flying boat with a small staff on 15 April. Unloading his poorly equipped and inexperienced British troops the next day, he immediately set them on the road to Trondheim.

On 19 April the French 5e Demi-Brigade Chasseurs Alpins also arrived, unloading from four large troopships. But, lacking motor transport, they were left behind while the British forces moved to Steinkjer (at the head of Beitstadfjord) and, having joined forces with a battalion of Norwegians, deployed into defensive positions around Vist. There they were immediately engaged by I/GJR 138 advancing out of Trondheim.

In a series of skirmishes over 21–22 April the mountain troops drove the British out of their positions while a small German flotilla landed another battalion of GJR 138 on their flank at Kirkenes. Meanwhile the Luftwaffe pounded Steinkjer and Namsos, ensuring the defeat was complete. The route to Trondheim thoroughly blocked, his forces in danger of encirclement and his supply base under merciless aerial attack, Carton de Wiart had no choice but to order a withdrawal and began planning to extricate his troops from the closing trap.

To form the southern arm of the pincer to retake Trondheim, the 148th Bde.'s two battalions were loaded aboard VAdm. Edward-Collins' cruisers and destroyers and transported across the North Sea on 17 April. Their role in the circular, indirect approach led to the unit being christened Sickleforce.

This contingent, under Brigadier Harold de R. Morgan, began unloading on the night of 18/19 April at Åndalsnes. Seven hundred and twenty-five Royal Marines landed from a flotilla of four AA sloops the previous day had secured this small port. Two companies of the 1st Bn./5th Leicestershire moved by train to Dombås to secure the important road/rail junction, arriving the day the German paratroopers surrendered.

In response to Gen.Maj. Ruge's request, Brig. Morgan's small force was diverted from its original mission. Abandoning the planned envelopment of Trondheim, two companies of 1st Bn./8th Sherwood Foresters travelled by train to just north of Lillehammer where Morgan established his brigade HQ.

By the time the British arrived at the front, it was split by the frozen Lake Mjøsa because the Norwegian withdrawals had pulled back along its east and west shores. On the east side, elements of the 5th Inf. Regt. held out at Strandlykkja for two days until a battalion of German troops (III/IR 362) outflanked them by marching across the frozen lake. Surprised and somewhat panicked, the Norwegian retreat was disorderly and precipitous, causing the next two defensive positions to be abandoned. On the western side of the lake, Col. Thor Dahl's single battalion of the 4th Inf. Regt. retreated as well, to Gjøvik, in fear of the same outflanking manoeuvre.

The first two companies of the Sherwood Foresters deployed to the west shore to reinforce Dahl's battered battalion at Biri while the rest of the Foresters relieved the Norwegian infantry in front of Lillehammer. The remaining two Leicestershire companies held the left flank at Åsmarka with the Norwegian Dragoons screening.

Approaching them, Pellengahr's advancing *Kampfgruppe* consisted of two battalions pushing northwards up the shorelines of Lake Mjøsa, supported by companies of engineers and motorized machine-gun troops, as well as six light and two heavy tanks. Additionally the Luftwaffe's control of the air was unchallenged; eight He 111s of II/KG 54 began aggressively pressing their attacks on the morning of 21 April, with Pellengahr launching his ground assaults at 1500hrs, just as the British were relieving the Norwegians in the forward positions.

Unseasoned, having limited ammunition, and no artillery, Morgan's men held out most of the day but were withdrawn to Fåberg during the night. The next morning the Germans renewed their assaults with air attacks, artillery barrages and two small tanks, easily outflanking the British and driving them out of their positions in disarray.

One last stand was made at Tretten Gorge on 23 April, with the battered, sleepless British soldiers now joined by the last two companies of the Leicestershire battalion. Tretten was the single most defensible position in the Gudbrandsdal and Ruge hoped that the British would be able to hold the Germans off for two or three days so he could strengthen his defences further north.

Pellengahr was an artillery expert and he used his field guns and howitzers with great skill. Shortly after noon two light tanks broke through the main British position while infantry infiltrated from the flank. Soon a large part of the British force was cut off while the Luftwaffe strafed those attempting to retreat. After nightfall an exhausted remnant of Morgan's unit finally escaped to the north, leaving 706 officers and men killed, missing or captured. The 148th Bde. had ceased to exist as a fighting unit.

To reinforce Sickleforce, the 15th Brigade was detached from the 5th Division in France and embarked for Norway on 15 April. Originally it was intended to be used in the direct naval/amphibious assault on Trondheim but this was cancelled four days later. This force consisted of three battalions – the 1st King's Own Yorkshire Light Infantry (1st KOYLI), 1st York and Lancaster (1st Y&L) and 1st Green Howards –

At Otta, Kampfgruppe Pellengahr prepares for the final push to oust Sickleforce from central Norway. Beyond this German mortar team it is easy to see the terrain in which the British set up their defensive positions. (Courtesy Imperial War Museum, London – HU93717)

▼ EVENTS

1. 20 APRIL: Norwegian infantry (II/IR 5) and dragoons (DR 2), under Obst. Jørgen Jensen, hold firm on the south slope of the Lundehögde against artillery bombardments and infantry attacks by IR 345 throughout the day. Gen.Lt. Pellengahr is reinforced by a motorized machine-gun battalion and prepares to renew the assaults the following day.

2. 20 APRIL: The first British unit to arrive and detrain at Fåberg, a half-battalion of 1st/8th Sherwood Foresters (A and D Coy, under Maj. J. K. L. Roberts), bivouac at Nykirke before deploying to defend the Bråstad Bridge, relieving the exhausted Norwegian I/IR 4. Two battalions of IR 324, with supporting troops, face them. Overall Allied commander is Obst. Thor A. Dahl.

148th ⊠
MORGAN

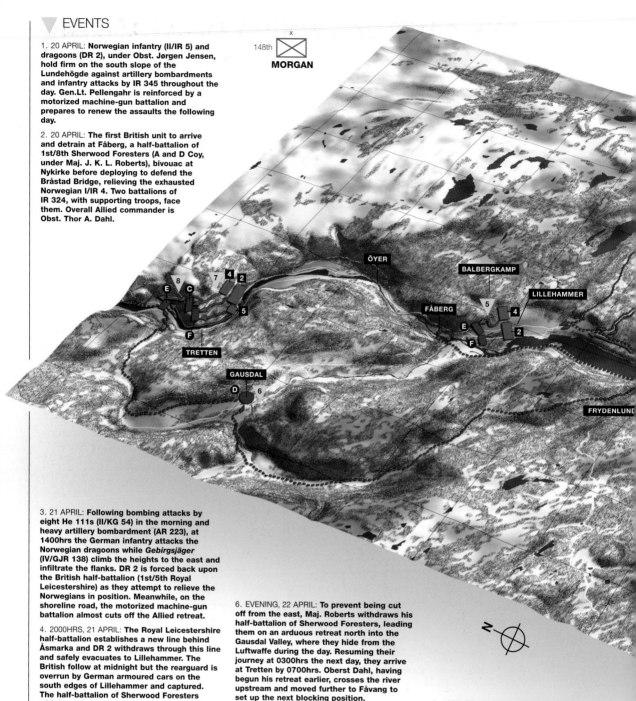

ÖYER

BALBERGKAMP

8 7 4 2
E C   LILLEHAMMER
                    5
        5   FÅBERG
F   E   4
TRETTEN   F   2

GAUSDAL

D 6   FRYDENLUND

3. 21 APRIL: Following bombing attacks by eight He 111s (II/KG 54) in the morning and heavy artillery bombardment (AR 223), at 1400hrs the German infantry attacks the Norwegian dragoons while *Gebirgsjäger* (IV/GJR 138) climb the heights to the east and infiltrate the flanks. DR 2 is forced back upon the British half-battalion (1st/5th Royal Leicestershire) as they attempt to relieve the Norwegians in position. Meanwhile, on the shoreline road, the motorized machine-gun battalion almost cuts off the Allied retreat.

4. 2000HRS, 21 APRIL: The Royal Leicestershire half-battalion establishes a new line behind Åsmarka and DR 2 withdraws through this line and safely evacuates to Lillehammer. The British follow at midnight but the rearguard is overrun by German armoured cars on the south edges of Lillehammer and captured. The half-battalion of Sherwood Foresters withdraw via an alternate route.

5. 22 APRIL: Now in command of his units and the Allied defensive positions north of Lillehammer, Brig. H. de R. Morgan deploys the half-battalion of Sherwood Foresters between the shoreline and the steep face of Balberg with the battered companies of the Royal Leicestershires as a second line of defence. The lines are hastily improvised and were attacked at midday along the shore road while German mountain troops scale the heights of the Balberg and falls upon the British flank and rear at 1530hrs, even attacking the 148th Bde. HQ, precipitating a further retreat up the valley.

6. EVENING, 22 APRIL: To prevent being cut off from the east, Maj. Roberts withdraws his half-battalion of Sherwood Foresters, leading them on an arduous retreat north into the Gausdal Valley, where they hide from the Luftwaffe during the day. Resuming their journey at 0300hrs the next day, they arrive at Tretten by 0700hrs. Oberst Dahl, having begun his retreat earlier, crosses the river upstream and moved further to Fåvang to set up the next blocking position.

7. 1030HRS, 23 APRIL: Brigadier Morgan's 148th Bde. makes its last stand south of Tretten Gorge. Two companies of Foresters and one of Leicesters cover the oblique shore road supported by the remaining Norwegian dragoons on the left flank. Major Robert's half-battalion protects the bridge and provides – along with the remaining Leicesters – the reserve. Following the successful format of previous engagements, at 1300hrs the Germans begin probing with infantry and bombarding with artillery while three tanks (1./Pz.-Abt. zbV 40) penetrate the British lines along the road. This threatens to close the British avenue of retreat.

8. 1800HRS, 23 APRIL: German mountain troops, having scaled the heights to the east, descend behind the Norwegian dragoons attacking 148th Bde. support troops in the rear. At 1900hrs a retreat is initiated but is hampered by air attacks, allowing German troops to close upon the forward British forces from all sides. A fighting withdrawal is attempted, but communications problems result in some units not disengaging while others are caught on the road by pursuing German armoured cars. Only 30 per cent of the 148th Bde. escapes destruction – most being captured – while the Norwegian infantry (I/IR 4) establishes a temporary blocking position at Fåvang.

THE BATTLES AROUND LILLEHAMMER, 20–24 APRIL 1940

Note: Gridlines are shown at intervals of 1km (1093yds)

GERMAN UNITS

1 Two battalions of Infanterie Regiment 324
2 Two battalions of Infanterie Regiment 345
3 One battery of artillery from Artillerie Regiment 223
4 Part of IV/Gebirgsjäger Regiment 138 (von Poncets)
5 One motorized machine-gun battalion, reinforced with one platoon of tanks

ALLIED UNITS

Norwegian

A One battalion of Infantry Regiment 4 (Obst. Thor A. Dahl)
B One battalion of Infantry Regiment 5 under the command of Dragoon Regiment 2 (Obst. Jørgen Jensen)
C Three squadrons of Dragoon Regiment 2

British

D One half-battalion of 1st/8th Sherwood Foresters (Maj. J. K. L. Roberts)
E One half-battalion of 1st/5th Royal Leicestershire Regt (Lt. Col. G. J. German)
F One half-battalion of 1st/8th Sherwood Foresters (Lt. Col. T. A. Ford)

under Brigadier H. E. F. Smyth. This brigade only consisted of infantry – plus one anti-tank gun company – because a U-boat sank the cargo ship bearing the brigade's motor transport, artillery, ammunition and rations while en route.

The brigade arrived at Åndalsnes on 23 April just as the 148th Bde. was being driven out of Tretten. The 15th Bde. headed south, passing the remains of the 148th Bde. and Norwegian 2nd Div., to establish a strong defensive position at Kvam, about 55km south of Dombås. To lead the enlarged Sickleforce was Major-General Bernard C. T. Paget, commander of the 18th Division in East Anglia.

Hardly had the 1st KOYLI deployed into position when the head of Pellengahr's leading column – one NbFz B heavy tank, one PzKpfw II light tank and an armoured car – came into sight and a brisk engagement developed. The brigade's five Hotchkiss 25mm anti-tank guns proved effective, knocking out the monstrous NbFz B and the little PzKpfw II, and the initial attacks were repulsed. Despite heavy artillery bombardment of their forward lines and infiltration from the flanks the British held out for two days. Threatened with encirclement, the battered British troops finally evacuated their positions after nightfall and fell back through Kjørem, where the 1st Y&L had prepared for the next defensive stand.

After a number of hard-fought engagements, each ending in retreat, Maj. Gen. Paget's assessment was that further defence in central Norway was completely untenable in the face of the Luftwaffe's air supremacy. He called for air support since the entire length of his supply line, as well as his base at Åndalsnes, was now under constant air attack. Although RAF fighters were on the way, they would not be enough.

THE LUFTWAFFE RULES THE AIR ... AND THE WAVES

The persistence of Norwegian resistance and the strength of the British response led quickly to a large increase in the Luftwaffe's involvement in the campaign, so much so that a larger command became necessary to coordinate the defences, offensive strikes, airlift operations and support services. Therefore Luftflotte 5 was formed on 12 April, with Göring giving command to Generaloberst Erhard Milch, the second highest officer in the Luftwaffe. Milch was a logistics and administrative expert. He quickly established Luftpark Oslo with 200 maintenance specialists to service and repair aircraft, a signals network to coordinate the disparate functions and three facilities repair columns using civilian personnel. On 16 April he moved the air fleet HQ from Hamburg to Oslo to be closer to the action.

Subordinate to Luftflotte 5, Fliegerkorps X provided area defence from Sola airfield with Bf 110 (I/ZG 76) and Ju 88C (Z./KG 30) Zerstörer, and moved Bf 109Es (II/JG 77) to Kristiansand's Kjevik airfield to protect Oslo Harbour and Fornebu Airfield from RAF bomber raids. Stukas (I/StG 1) and He 111s (KG 26) mounted anti-shipping strikes from Sola while Hs 129 army observation aircraft (2(H)/10) and other He 111s (KG 4) supported Pellengahr's advance northwards. In addition,

Fliegerkorps X was supplied with one *Gruppe* of long-range Ju 87R Stukas. The pinpoint accuracy of dive-bombing proved especially effective against RN warships and transports penned in the narrow fjords. (Courtesy Imperial War Museum, London – HU2924)

HMS *Suffolk*'s bombardment of Sola Airfield had no effect on Fliegerkorps X's anti-shipping abilities. Hit twice in 82 attacks the cruiser limped into Scapa Flow its quarterdeck awash. (Courtesy Imperial War Museum, London – HU49670)

towards the middle of the month Geisler was assigned two *Gruppen* of Ju 88As (II and III(K)/LG 1), two of He 111s (I and II/KG 54) and one squadron (1./KG 40) of new four-engine FW 200C maritime patrol bombers to assist in curbing the operations of the Royal Navy.

The British response to this was meagre by comparison, with RAF Bomber Command attempting to neutralize Sola and Fornebu airfields by unescorted air attacks, which were inevitably decimated by German fighters and flak, losing 31 bombers in 576 sorties in the first month of operations. In a desperate effort to close Sola's operations, the Home Fleet sent HMS *Suffolk* and four destroyers to bombard the airfield.

Arriving before dawn on 17 April, the heavy cruiser launched its Walrus seaplane to illuminate the target with flares, but a Ju 88C Zerstörer promptly shot this down. Consequently the bombardment had little accuracy or effect and, after sunrise, the Luftwaffe responded with 82 bomber sorties as the cruiser attempted to escape. In the seven-hour ordeal it was hit twice and finally slipped into Scapa Flow in a near-sinking condition.

The only real way to counter the power of the Luftwaffe was to base RAF fighters on Norwegian soil. But this effort was so pitifully small it was doomed from the start.

THE NBFZ B 'HEAVY TANK' IN THE BATTLE OF KVAM, 25 APRIL 1940 (pages 66–67)

Having practically destroyed the British 148th Brigade in the battles around Lillehammer and swept away the weak Norwegian forces at Fåvang and Ringebu, Generalleutnant Pellengahr's column marched north through the Gudbrandsdal as if on parade. Leading the procession was one of the three operational NbFz B (also known as PzKpfw VI) heavy tanks in the German army (1). Specifically designed as an infantry support vehicle, the 35-ton 'land battleship' sported three turrets – the main turret carrying coaxially mounted 37mm and 75mm guns along with a small machine-gun turret fore and aft for close-in defence. Supporting this behemoth was a single PzKpfw II light tank (2) and an SdKfz 231 armoured car (3). Behind this vanguard came the procession of lorried infantry, truck-towed artillery and marching troops. On 25 April, as the column emerged from the narrower defiles of the Lågen River (4) they saw the valley open up into gently sloping farmlands sweeping up the sides of the evergreen-capped ridge on the right and the broad, flat Viksöy Island,

fringed with willows, on the left. Hidden in the trees on both flanks – with excellent fields of fire covering the roadway – were A and B Companies of 1st Bn., KOYLI, each with a Hotchkiss 25mm A/T gun (5). When the leading vehicles of the German column came inside a quarter mile, A Coy unleashed the first shot from their concealed position on Viksöy Island, disabling the NbFz B with a hit on its running gear. The escorting PzKpfw II manoeuvred around the disabled heavy tank only to be knocked out by the second round from A Coy's gun. The SdKfz 231 beat a hasty retreat and the column behind came to a halt. Though immobilized the NbFz B fought on, using its 37mm and 75mm guns against A Coy on Viksöy Island while behind it the Germans unloaded from their lorries, unlimbered their artillery and deployed for a more traditional advance and assaults. Using artillery barrages and flanking manoeuvres they attacked British positions throughout the rest of the day. The KOYLI fought doggedly and, withdrawing slowly and begrudgingly, they held up Pellengahr's advance for two full days, finally vacating the field at 1800hrs on 26 April.

With no suitable airfields in the area, No. 263 Squadron's Gloster Gladiators were forced to operate from the frozen surface of Lake Lesjaskog. Their exposure to enemy attack is obvious. (Courtesy Imperial War Museum, London – HU2874)

Since there were no suitable airfields in the region, the frozen Lake Lesjaskog, located in the broad valley between Åndalsnes and Dombås, approximately 80km south of the former, was selected as the best possible operating location. No. 263 Squadron, consisting of 18 Gladiator IIs led by Squadron Leader John W. 'Baldy' Donaldson, sailed from Orkney on 20 April aboard HMS *Glorious* and, four days later, the Gladiators arrived at their forward base and began setting up for combat operations.

What they found were severely primitive conditions and an almost total absence of support. There were no facilities with all work having to be done in the open, exposed to attack. The machine guns had to be reloaded by hand, the airplanes refuelled using milk jugs acquired from nearby farmers, and there was no acid for the batteries of the starter cart. The unit was soon discovered by the Luftwaffe, which quickly shifted its efforts to destroy the impudent British force.

Completely lacking an early warning system, with aircraft parked in the open, the unit was hit repeatedly by German bomber formations attacking at regular intervals for eight continuous hours. Between attacks, at 1000hrs on 25 April, the unit launched its most significant mission when six Gladiators flew top cover over the frontline troops at Kvam for two hours. However, returning to Lake Lesjaskog they found their base under attack yet again and shot down one He 111 as they chased the raiders away.

During the afternoon subsequent sorties destroyed two He 111s but the continued air raids destroyed all but five Gladiators on the ground. By the end of the day Sqn. Ldr. Donaldson realized that the base was untenable and withdrew the unit to Stetnesmeon, the Norwegian Army depot near Åndalsnes. With their fuel stocks exhausted, the following day the last three Gladiators were burned and the men and what little equipment could be saved were moved to Åndalsnes for re-embarkment.

For anti-aircraft defence the RN put its faith in AA guns: high-angle 4in. for barrage fire against level bombers and quad-mounted .5in. machine guns for close-in defence against dive-bombers. In addition to mounting these on many warships, the RN developed dedicated AA cruisers (eight 4in. guns) and destroyer-size AA sloops (six 4in. guns) to defend the fleet and its anchorages. However, against dive-bombing

By the end of the day over a dozen Gladiators and six Skuas had been destroyed by the Luftwaffe's relentless air attacks. (Courtesy Imperial War Museum, London – HU2873)

British AA cruisers and sloops attempted to defend Allied ports of embarkation, and frequently took the brunt of the air attacks. Here AA sloop HMS *Bittern* burns following a Stuka strike. (Courtesy Imperial War Museum, London – N64)

attacks the rate of fire of the 4in. guns proved too slow, while the machine guns' lethal envelope was too small. In the battle developing in the Åndalsnes and Namsos fjords between dive-bombers and dedicated AA ships, the latter came out second best.

Once Luftwaffe reconnaissance discovered that the two small ports were used as Allied supply bases, they were mercilessly and effectively bombed in spite of the dedicated AA ships stationed in the harbours. The defending vessels suffered as well, HMS *Bittern* at Namsos was damaged so badly by a Ju 87R on 30 April that she had to be sunk by torpedo. Two other AA sloops and one AA cruiser were so damaged they had to sail home for repairs. Additionally, the remaining vessels fired off so much 4in. and machine-gun ammunition that stocks were critically low and gun barrels were worn smooth, reducing accuracy even more. During the 1,050 bombing sorties flown against the two ports only nine German bombers were shot down by AA fire.

While the Luftwaffe was annihilating their meagre air defences, the 15th Bde. again attempted to stop the irresistible German advance at

Luftwaffe bombers were mainly used for interdiction, bombing British supply dumps, Norwegian railway lines and the Allies' routes of retreat. (Courtesy Imperial War Museum, London – HU93726)

Kjørem. The Germans attacked on the morning of 27 April and, after holding out for a day, the British were forced to retire to Otta, 20km to the rear. There, the following day, the Green Howards made a determined stand, inflicting heavy casualties on the attacking Germans, including knocking out three more tanks. When they withdrew that evening, Pellengahr made no move to pursue.

Meanwhile in Østerdal, Obst. Fischer's *Kampfgruppe* had made steady progress against weak Norwegian resistance and, on 26 April, was at Alvdal (only 96km north-east of Dombås) threatening the Allies from the rear. Three days later Fischer linked up with forces out of Trondheim, making the outcome obvious.

With Sickleforce unprotected against Luftwaffe air attacks, threatened from the rear and hopelessly outgunned at the front, on 28 April the War Cabinet finally ordered the British expeditionary forces evacuated, leaving the Norwegians devastated by the news since they had been counting on increased British support, not less.

Despite constant pounding by air attacks Maj. Gen. Paget successfully extricated his forces from a hopelessly losing situation, re-embarking on RN cruisers and destroyers on 30 April and 1 May, with the last of the rearguard evacuated the following night. King Håkon and members of the Norwegian government were evacuated from Mølde the first night – bound for Tromsø in the far north – with Gen.Maj. Ruge and his staff departing the next day. Generalmajor Hvinden-Haug surrendered the remnants of the Norwegian 2nd Division on 3 May.

Miraculously, while Sickleforce had lost 1,301 men killed, missing or captured in ground combat, a total of 5,084 were safely evacuated with no losses at sea.

Mauriceforce, evacuating Namsos on much the same schedule, was not so lucky. Following the withdrawal from Steinkjer the British fell back towards the port and established a defence in depth along the

route. The Germans, however, were satisfied that they had sealed off the northern threat to Trondheim and dug in around Steinkjer to prevent a renewed Allied advance.

Without pressure from ground forces, Mauriceforce's evacuation was impeded only by the weather. Fog in the fjord limited the first night's embarkation to only a single battalion of 850 French *Chasseurs alpins*, so the remaining 5,350 troops had to be loaded the second night, 2/3 May. The rearguard boarded HMS *Afridi* at 0430hrs, as the sun was rising, and the destroyer tarried long enough to shell the force's motor transport, which was crowded on the quay, before setting off to rejoin the evacuation fleet.

At 0945hrs formations of He 111s and Ju 88s arrived over the fleet and air attacks began, concentrating at first on the cruisers *Devonshire* and *Montcalm*. These were missed, but two hours into the assault the large French destroyer *Bison* was hit, disabled and set afire. The 2,645-ton ship had to be abandoned, with its crew transferring to three attending RN destroyers, *Afridi* among them. Stukas arrived a short time later and *Afridi* was next to be hit, being damaged amidships and in the hull. Foundering, she too was abandoned with the loss of 100 men, 30 of whom were recently rescued French sailors.

The loss of *Afridi* added another 14 soldiers lost at sea to the 153 killed, missing and captured that Mauriceforce experienced in ground combat. Far more important was the fact that two British forces, totalling more than a division, had been beaten in combat and driven from the land they were there to save, largely by the Germans' monopoly of air power. The Luftwaffe had been decisive in the outcome of the fighting in central Norway.

TRAPPED AT NARVIK

As Allied efforts in central Norway were overwhelmed by the German forces, steady progress was being made in the north to retake Narvik. The 24th Bde. began landing at Harstad, some 55km from Narvik, on 14 April after Maj. Gen. Mackesy negotiated the consent of Generalmajor Carl G. Fleischer, who commanded the Norwegian 6th Division. The

brigade's three battalions were spread out among several locations to protect the main landing area, the RN fleet anchorage and other rear areas, freeing Norwegian units to fight the Germans.

Major-General Mackesy was faithful to his orders to establish a base from which a ground advance upon Narvik could be launched. Unfortunately this design was diametrically opposed to Whitehall's – and the overall commander's – desire for an immediate amphibious landing at Narvik. Consequently Gen.Lt. Dietl was given plenty of time to incorporate 1,600 sailors, organize his defences and be reinforced by air.

Dietl's forces enclosed a rather large perimeter with two battalions arrayed along the northern front and the third defending against approaches along the shores of Ofotfjord and Beisfjord. The naval regiment was armed with some of the 8,000 rifles and 315 machine guns captured at the Elvegårdsmoen depot and was spread along the fjord shorelines to prevent an Allied amphibious assault. They also defended the length of the railway line where it tracked along the south shore of Rombaksfjord from Narvik to Sildvik.

Within this spacious perimeter was the Kuberg Plateau and Lake Hartvigvatn, both with relatively flat, open areas conducive to airborne operations. In fact, on 13 April ten Ju 52/3m transports (3./KGrzbV 102) landed on the frozen lake, bringing in a four-gun battery (2./GAR 112) of 75mm mountain howitzers. However, only one was able to fly out again; four were destroyed by Norwegian and FAA air attacks and the others were stranded as a result of damage, lack of fuel and the ice breaking up.

In addition Lufttransportchef Land organized an additional 387 airlift sorties, basing 85 Ju 52/3ms at Trondheim's Værnes airfield, dropping a total of 528 troops, including a battalion of *Fallschirmjäger* (II/FJR 2) fresh from their combats in Holland as well as 66 *Gebirgsjäger* who had hastily completed a ten-day parachuting course. These were supplemented by deliveries of men, equipment, ammunition and supplies by the transport seaplanes of KGrzbV 108. Thirteen additional transports were lost in this airlift operation.

On 23 April, the Norwegian 6th Brigade began an offensive to compress the German perimeter and retake Narvik. While their attacks

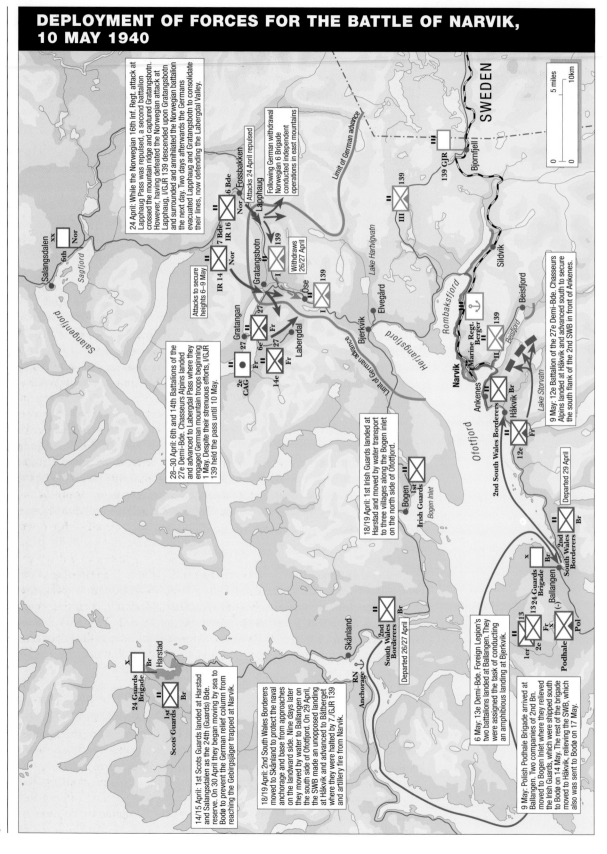

24 April: While the Norwegian 16th Inf. Regt. attack at Lapphaug Pass was repulsed, a second battalion crossed the mountain ridge and captured Gratangsbotn. However, having defeated the Norwegian attack at Lapphaug, I/GJR 139 descended upon Gratangsbotn and surrounded and annihilated the Norwegian battalion the next day. Two days afterwards the Germans evacuated Lapphaug and Gratangsbotn to consolidate their lines, now defending the Labergdal Valley.

28–30 April: 6th and 14th Battalions of the 27e Demi-Bde. Chasseurs Alpins landed and advanced to Labergdal Pass where they engaged German mountain troops beginning 1 May. Despite their strenuous efforts, I/GJR 139 held the pass until 10 May.

18/19 April: 1st Irish Guards landed at Harstad and moved by water transport to three villages along the Bogen inlet on the north side of Ofotfjord.

14/15 April: 1st Scots Guards landed at Harstad and Salangsdalen as the 24th (Guards) Bde. reserve. On 30 April they began moving by sea to Bodø to prevent the German relief column from reaching the Gebirgsjäger trapped at Narvik.

18/19 April: 2nd South Wales Borderers moved to Skånland to protect the naval anchorage and base from approaches on the landward side. Nine days later they moved by water to Ballangen on the south side of Ofotfjord. On 29 April, the SWB made an unopposed landing at Håkvik and advanced to Båtberget where they were halted by 7./GJR 139 and artillery fire from Narvik.

6 May: 13e Demi-Bde. Foreign Legion's two battalions landed at Ballangen. They were assigned the task of conducting an amphibious landing at Bjerkvik.

9 May: Polish Podhale Brigade arrived at Ballangen. Two companies of 2nd Bn. moved to Bogen Inlet where they relieved the Irish Guards, which were shipped south to Bodø on 14 May. The rest of the brigade moved to Håkvik, relieving the SWB, which also was sent to Bodø on 17 May.

9 May: 12e Battalion of the 27e Demi-Bde. Chasseurs Alpins landed at Håkvik and advanced south to secure the south flank of the 2nd SWB in front of Ankenes.

9 May: 1st Battalion of the 27e Demi-Bde. Chasseurs Alpins landed at Håkvik and advanced south to secure the south flank of the 2nd SWB in front of Ankenes.

74

Meanwhile Allied forces were continually reinforced. Here Polish troops are briefed aboard a Norwegian coastal steamer before going ashore to push the Germans out of Ankenes. (Courtesy Imperial War Museum, London – HU93734)

at Lapphaug Pass were repulsed, a second battalion crossed the mountain range to the west and captured Gratangsbotn behind the German lines. However, a snowstorm intervened, suspending the attacks in the mountain pass and allowing the Germans to descend upon Gratangsbotn and retake it. Thereafter a stalemate ensued.

Lord Cork and Orrery still believed a direct assault on Narvik itself was practicable and put it to a test on 24 April when British warships – the battleship *Warspite*, three cruisers and a destroyer – steamed into Ofotfjord and bombarded the town to provide a diversion for the Norwegian offensive in Lapphaug Pass. In case the opportunity arose Mackesy had embarked the Irish Guards on the repair ship *Vindictive* to go ashore and secure the port. In snowy, tempestuous conditions the bombardment had little effect and German surrender did not occur. However, Lord Cork did have the occasion to go ashore at an undefended stretch of coastline and was soon convinced that troops landing from open boats and attempting to advance uphill in hip-deep snow would have been suicidal.

Despite their victories at Lapphaug and Gratangsbotn two days prior, the Germans evacuated both positions on 26/27 April to shorten their lines. The same day the British finally moved towards contact with the enemy, the 2nd South Wales Borderers sailing to Ballangen on the south side of Ofotfjord, approximately 16km west of Narvik. Three days later they travelled by water to Håkvik and advanced along the shore road to Båtberget (2.5km west of Ankenes) where they were halted by German machine-gun positions and artillery fire from Narvik.

On 28 April the 27e Demi-Brigade Chasseurs Alpins arrived, the 12e Bn. moving to Håkvik on 9 May and manning a series of outposts from Håkvik to Lake Storvatn to protect the Borderers' south flank. The energetic, dynamic and aggressive Gén. de bde. Béthouart led the French, and he was eager to come to grips with the enemy. His other two battalions, the 6e and 14e, joined the Norwegians in the north and, supported by the 2e Groupe Autonome d'Artillerie Coloniale, they began attacking the German positions at Labergdal Pass on 4 May. The terrain and weather made the effort strenuous and difficult, but the Germans finally gave up the position six days later.

Precursor to D-Day: British landing craft conduct the Allies' first amphibious assault of World War II, landing French legionnaires to retake Bjerkvik from the Germans. (Courtesy Imperial War Museum, London – HU93723)

By this time the contest for central Norway was complete and Fliegerkorps X began to move its forces to Trondheim's Værnes airfield to resume the battle between bombers and ships. The first unit based there was the pathfinder KGr 100, which flew its first mission to the Narvik area on 4 May and sank the 2,144-ton Polish destroyer *Grom* with the loss of 65 crewmen. Two groups of He 111 bombers (I and III/KG 26) and one of long-range Stukas (I/StG 1) soon followed them.

However, these could not stop the continued flow of Allied troops and on 6 May the French Légion Étranger's13e Demi-Brigade arrived, followed three days later by the Polish Podhale Brigade. The Poles took up positions replacing the South Wales Borderers at Båtberget, facing the Germans at Ankenes, while the legionnaires at Ballangen prepared for the Allies' first real amphibious assault of the war.

Béthouart's plan was first to occupy the northern shore of Ofotfjord, opposite Narvik, and subsequently launch a cross-fjord assault into Narvik itself. Beginning at midnight – which was still daylight at that latitude – on 12/13 May the battleship *Resolution*, two cruisers and five destroyers began shelling the planned assault area 1km west of Bjerkvik, targeting German machine-gun posts along the shore, setting houses ablaze and blowing up ammunition stocks.

After an hour's bombardment the small amphibious flotilla passed the warships: four Assault Landing Craft (ALCs) bearing one company of legionnaires (1er Bn., 13e DBLE) and one Motor Landing Craft (MLC) carrying a Hotchkiss H-39 light tank (342e Compagnie Autonome de Chars de Combat). These were joined by two 'boat chains' consisting of one motor whaler towing two large ship's boats bearing another 120-man company. Abeam their landing point the column of boats turned in towards shore and ran themselves aground, disgorging the tank and troops. Joined by two more MLCs landing H-39 tanks, and reinforced by the remaining two companies an hour later, the legionnaires silenced the German resistance along the shore and advanced upon Bjerkvik from the west.

The second wave – the 2e Bn. of legionnaires and two additional tanks – landed at 0300hrs approximately 600m south of Bjerkvik, forming the southern arm of a pincer movement against the German stronghold. The

Two things were expected to change the complexion of the Narvik operation: a new commander in Major-General Auchinleck and the RAF, represented here by its component commander, Group Captain M. Moore, in conference aboard SS *Chrobry*. (Courtesy Imperial War Museum, London – N134)

HMS *Effingham* ready to sail to Bodø carrying the South Wales Borderers. She was lost en route with all their equipment, including these Bren carriers embarked on deck. (Courtesy Imperial War Museum, London – N249)

main body of the battalion advanced upon Elvegårdsmoen depot and captured it in fierce building-by-building fighting, driving the German defenders out to the east. The battalion's motorcycle section drove south and secured Øyjord. From there they could look across the still waters of Ofotfjord at their ultimate objective, Narvik.

Also on 13 May, Maj. Gen. Claude J. E. Auchinleck arrived to replace the deliberate but disappointing Mackesy. Based on Mackesy's plans and dispositions, Auchinleck could see no way of speeding up the advance on Narvik, but he could also see that Béthouart's troops were the best equipped and trained for the job. Additionally there was the worrisome advance of GR 138, now reinforced by Generalleutnant Valentin Feuerstein's 2.Gebirgs-Division recently landed at Trondheim and approaching from the south to relieve Dietl. Turning the Narvik enterprise over to the French brigadier, Auchinleck began shuttling battalions of the 24th Bde. south to Bodø to stem the relentlessly advancing Germans.

This operation was plagued with misfortune. While the Scots Guards – along with four 25-pdr and four light AA guns – departed aboard the

▼ EVENTS

1. BEGINNING 12 MAY: The Norwegian 6th Brigade begins to move up the north slope of the Kuberg Plateau. The German line is steadily driven back over two weeks of heavy fighting in deep snow.

2. 13 MAY: The 13e Demi-Bde. de Légion Étranger lands two battalions, recapturing Bjerkvik and Elevgårdsmoen in heavy fighting. The unit's motorcycle section races south to secure Seines and Øyjord, the starting points for the final assault on Narvik.

3. 13 MAY: The 27e Demi-Bde. de Chasseurs Alpins pushes German *Gebirgsjäger* out of Labergdal Pass and, advancing south, links up with the legionnaires before continuing to drive to Lilleberget and Nygård.

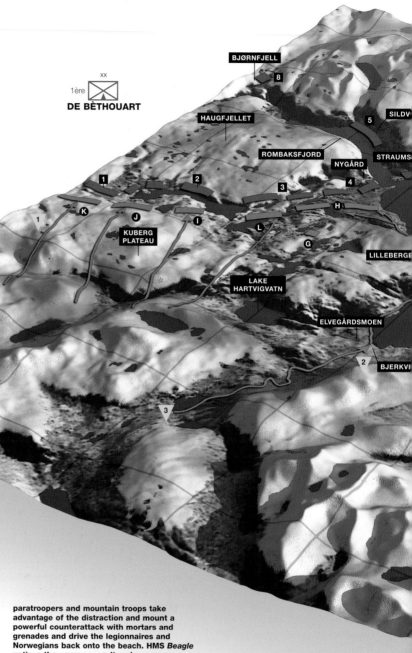

1ère XX DE BÈTHOUART

BJØRNFJELL
HAUGFJELLET
SILDV
ROMBAKSFJORD
NYGÅRD
STRAUMS
KUBERG PLATEAU
LAKE HARTVIGVATN
LILLEBERGE
ELVEGÅRDSMOEN
BJERKVI

GERMAN UNITS

Gruppe Windisch
1   I/GJR 139
2   III/GJR 139
3   III/GJR 138 (minus two companies)
4   Marine-Bataillon Kothe

Marine-Regiment Berger
5   Marine-Bataillon Thiele
6   Marine-Bataillon Holtorf
7   Marine-Bataillon Zenker
8   Marine-Bataillon Arnim

Gruppe Narvik
9   II/GJR 139 (minus two companies)
10   I/FJR 1
11   2./GAR 112
12   Marine-Bataillon Freytag-Loringhofen
13   7./GJR 139
14   8./GJR 139

---

4. 2330HRS, 28 MAY: HMS *Cairo* and four destroyers begin bombarding Orneset Beach, supported by French and Norwegian artillery at Øyjord. At midnight five RN assault landing craft from Seines round the Øyjord Point and cross the fjord, landing two companies of legionnaires (1er Bn./13e DBLE) and two H-39 tanks on Orneset Beach. The tanks quickly bog down, but the legionnaires push the Germans up to the railway line, securing the beach for subsequent waves.

5. 0100HRS, 28 MAY: While the assault craft return to the north shore to pick up II/IR 15, German 75mm guns (2./GAR 112) atop Taraldsvik Ridge drive them into Herjangsfjord, necessitating embarkation at Seines. Arriving late, the Norwegians land on the right flank of the legionnaires and begin pushing the Germans uphill.

6. 0430HRS, 28 MAY: Just after dawn, two waves of Luftwaffe bombers – six Ju 88s (II/KG 30) and 26 He 111s (KG 26 and KGr 100) – arrive to disrupt the landings. RAF fighters intercept them and four bombers are shot down. But they damage HMS *Cairo* and cause RN warships to discontinue bombardment and manoeuvre to prevent being hit. At Orneset Beach the German

paratroopers and mountain troops take advantage of the distraction and mount a powerful counterattack with mortars and grenades and drive the legionnaires and Norwegians back onto the beach. HMS *Beagle* notices the enemy assault and resumes bombardment, breaking the German counterattack.

7. 0000HRS, 27/28 MAY: At Ankenes the Polish 2e Bn. attacks, supported by two H-39 tanks, RA 25-pdrs and HMS *Southampton's* gunfire. Despite the support, the attack is repulsed and a seesaw battle develops with a ferocious German counterattack at 0700hrs. However, by noon the Poles have stabilized the situation and as the heights above the town are taken the Germans retreat to Nyborg and evacuate in small boats. The Poles' 1er Bn. pushes down the ridgeline and descended upon Beisfjord village to cut off the German escape route.

8. 0700HRS, 28 MAY: After the Luftwaffe air attacks, the legionnaires' 2e Bn. and three more H-39s are landed on the right flank of Orneset Beach and begin pushing towards Narvik, about midday taking the northern heights overlooking the railway station. After a day of hard fighting, Maj. Haussels decides the town can no longer be defended and orders the German units to retreat overland to the east. At 1700hrs the Norwegian troops enter Narvik. Meanwhile the legionnaires' motorcycle section races down to Beisfjord village to link up with the advancing Polish Brigade.

ALLIED FORCES RECAPTURE NARVIK, 12–28 MAY

Note: Gridlines are shown at intervals of 1km (1093yds)

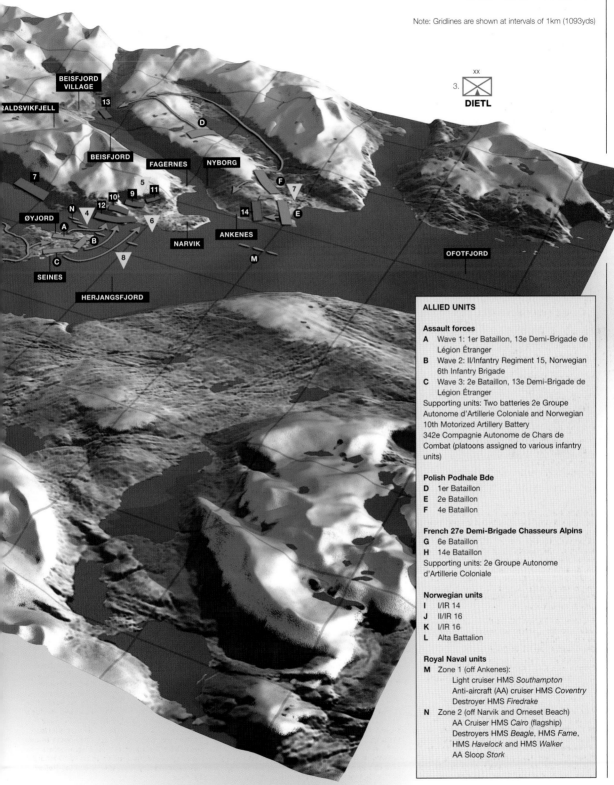

3. XX DIETL

ALLIED UNITS

Assault forces

A Wave 1: 1er Bataillon, 13e Demi-Brigade de Légion Étranger

B Wave 2: II/Infantry Regiment 15, Norwegian 6th Infantry Brigade

C Wave 3: 2e Bataillon, 13e Demi-Brigade de Légion Étranger

Supporting units: Two batteries 2e Groupe Autonome d'Artillerie Coloniale and Norwegian 10th Motorized Artillery Battery

342e Compagnie Autonome de Chars de Combat (platoons assigned to various infantry units)

Polish Podhale Bde

D 1er Bataillon

E 2e Bataillon

F 4e Bataillon

French 27e Demi-Brigade Chasseurs Alpins

G 6e Bataillon

H 14e Bataillon

Supporting units: 2e Groupe Autonome d'Artillerie Coloniale

Norwegian units

I I/IR 14

J II/IR 16

K I/IR 16

L Alta Battalion

Royal Naval units

M Zone 1 (off Ankenes):
Light cruiser HMS *Southampton*
Anti-aircraft (AA) cruiser HMS *Coventry*
Destroyer HMS *Firedrake*

N Zone 2 (off Narvik and Orneset Beach)
AA Cruiser HMS *Cairo* (flagship)
Destroyers HMS *Beagle*, HMS *Fame*, HMS *Havelock* and HMS *Walker*
AA Sloop *Stork*

light cruiser HMS *Enterprise* on 11 May to support the five Independent Companies (Scissorforce) of commandos at Mo i Rana and Mosjøen, the others were not so lucky. On 15 May, en route to Bodø the 11,442-ton troopship *Chrobry* carrying the 1st Irish Guards was attacked and sunk by six He 111s (I/KG 26), killing the battalion commander and five staff officers and taking to the bottom the only three Vickers Mark VI light tanks assigned to the expedition. Similarly the heavy cruiser *Effingham* embarked the South Wales Borderers but, taking a shortcut to avoid enemy bombers, ran hard aground at 20 knots and had to be abandoned; the troops were taken off without their equipment, including some Bren carriers. Meanwhile the approaching Germans used the same tactics they had perfected in central Norway to drive back the British troops in engagement after engagement. The British finally evacuated Bodø on 31 May.

Meanwhile north of Narvik, the fall of Bjerkvik caused the collapse of the German perimeter. The Norwegian 6th Brigade, supported by Fokker C.V-D light bombers of the Hågoland Flyavdeling, had been attacking for two days, pushing up the north slope of the Kuberg Plateau in deep (2–3m) snow. The German line, consisting of machine-gun nests spaced as much as 1km apart and supported by a thin line of observation posts, was infiltrated and driven back.

In concert with the landings on the 13th, the French 27e DBCA, supported by their colonial artillery and the Norwegian 7th Brigade, attacked German positions south of Labergdal Pass. These finally gave way when it was learned that the Allies had taken Bjerkvik in their rear and the *Gebirgsjäger* withdrew to the south-east allowing the *Chasseurs alpins* to link up with the legionnaires the following morning.

As Béthouart consolidated his positions on the north shore of Ofotfjord, he completed the preparations for the cross-fjord assault to re-take Narvik itself. At this point the only thing that could save Dietl's embattled battalions was the Luftwaffe. But by this time, after 21 May, the situation changed because No. 263 Squadron returned to Norway with another 18 Gladiator IIs augmented by No. 46 Squadron with 18 Hawker Hurricane Is, both these units being based at Bardufoss.

However, the RAF lacked an effective early warning network resulting in late scrambles to intercept the German raiders. Consequently, the battle between bombers and ships resumed in Ofotfjord and the Skånland anchorage, with the RN warships continuing to take a beating. On 26 May the AA cruiser *Curlew* succumbed to KGr 100 bombers at Skånland.

Beginning at 2340hrs on 27 May, four RN destroyers in Rombaksfjord began shelling the planned assault area just 1.5km east of Narvik, targeting German machine-gun posts along the shore and hidden in railroad tunnel openings. From Øyjord two French and one Norwegian batteries of 75mm guns also bombarded the landing zone. The RAF squadrons were grounded due to fog at Bardufoss.

At midnight – but in broad daylight – three ALCs and two MLCs delivered 290 legionnaires (1er Bn., 13e DBLE) and two H-39 light tanks to the shore. The tanks bogged down, but the legionnaires pushed doggedly uphill as the landing craft returned to Herjangsfjord for the next wave. The 2nd Battalion of the Norwegian 15th Infantry Regt., a unit drawn largely from the Narvik area, followed the legionnaires ashore, landing on their right flank and began fighting to capture the high ground covering the eastern approach to their hometown.

By 0400hrs the beachhead was secured, but the Norwegians and legionnaires were heavily engaged in a see-saw battle as the German troops counterattacked with mortars and hand grenades. Barrages from the destroyer *Beagle* and the field guns at Øyjord finally broke this assault. Meanwhile Luftwaffe air attacks forced the British warships to discontinue bombardment and manoeuvre to dodge bombs. One Norwegian fishing boat ferrying ammunition was blown up and HMS *Cairo* was hit twice, suffering 30 casualties. The raids also delayed the landing of the 2e Bn. of legionnaires, allowing Dietl's remaining troops to escape to the east, retiring up the ore railway towards Bjornfjell.

By 1700hrs the victory was won and the Allies turned west to enter the city. Graciously Béthouart allowed the Norwegians, led by Gen.Maj. Fleischer, the honour of entering Narvik first.

From the bridge of HMS *Cairo* Général de brigade Béthouart monitors the progress of the assault on Narvik. (Courtesy Imperial War Museum, London – HU93730)

THE FINAL ACT – OPERATION *JUNO*

Since the Luftwaffe could not prevent the Allies from recapturing Narvik and pressing Dietl's forces back against the Swedish frontier, Grossadmiral Raeder hoped that the remaining heavy warships of his Kriegsmarine could. Thus *Weserübung* ended as it began, with a German naval foray, in this case Operation *Juno*.

As early as 14 May, the day Guderian's Panzers crossed the Meuse and broke through French lines at Sedan, the SKL had proposed to sortie the *Gneisenau, Scharnhorst* and *Admiral Hipper* to attack British shipping off Harstad. A week later Raeder suggested the concept to Hitler as a means of relieving the pressure on Narvik. By this time Guderian's drive to the sea had sealed the fate of France and Operation *Dynamo*, the evacuation of the BEF from Dunkirk, was in full cry. Emboldened by his amazing feat of arms, Hitler consented and the sortie was scheduled for 4 June.

The precipitous collapse of the Western Front had a decisive effect on the Allies as well. On 24 May the British War Cabinet, now headed by Winston Churchill as Prime Minister (the Chamberlain government having fallen two weeks prior as a result of the failure in central Norway), decided to abandon Norway. Lord Cork and Maj. Gen. Auchinleck were informed that day and passed the depressing news to Béthouart. The French commander bravely elected to go ahead with the final move to recapture Narvik in spite of the ongoing agony of his country's defeat. However, as soon as Narvik was secure and Dietl was driven back into a 260km² perimeter around Bjornfjell, the evacuation of 24,500 Allied troops began. In charge of the shipping was Rear-Admiral John G. P. Vivian, commanding the 20th (AA) Cruiser Squadron. He organized the available vessels into three convoys: a slow one of storeships and two groups of faster troop transports.

The first group of troopships berthed in various inlets and small fjords while the troops were brought to them in destroyers and Norwegian fishing vessels, mainly at night to escape detection by the Luftwaffe. This process took three nights and the six fast liners steamed out of Andfjord on 6 June with almost 15,000 Allied troops aboard, followed the next day by the slow convoy. Admiral Sir Charles Forbes dispatched the battleship *Valiant* and four destroyers to shepherd these two convoys across the North Sea while the second group of liners loaded.

Of the second group, the 19,840-ton liner *Orama* was short of fuel oil and water, and proved to be excess to Vivian's needs. It was sent home without escort in the company of the hospital ship *Atlantis*, while the other seven ships moved into the fjords to embark the remaining troops.

The two RAF squadrons at Bardufoss were evacuated as well. Having flown 638 sorties and shot down 14 enemy aircraft, Nos. 46 and No. 263 Squadrons were now down to ten fighters each. HMS *Glorious* arrived offshore with a reduced air group so it could accommodate the score of RAF aircraft. In an extraordinary feat of airmanship the RAF pilots landed all 20 aeroplanes safely aboard the carrier on 8 June. Immediately, Captain Guy D'Oyly Hughes, his ship escorted by two older destroyers, headed back to Scapa Flow.

Although the Luftwaffe continued to raid Allied shipping near Narvik – as seen here with HMS *Vindictive* under attack – they failed to notice the evacuation was well underway. (Courtesy Imperial War Museum, London – N248)

The empty troopship *Orama* goes down as German destroyer *Hans Lody* stands by to rescue survivors. (Courtesy Imperial War Museum, London – LN13573)

Amazingly, in spite of regular Luftwaffe reconnaissance, the evacuation of nearly 25,000 troops, almost all their heavy equipment and two RAF squadrons escaped the Germans' notice.

Because the ongoing evacuation was unknown when Adm. Wilhelm Marschall sailed from Kiel on 4 June, he was ordered to attack Allied shipping at Harstad. His force consisted of the two battlecruisers, one heavy cruiser, four destroyers and two torpedo boats. They slipped out of the Skaggerak and steamed northwards, rendezvousing three days later with the tanker *Dithmarschen* to refuel the *Hipper* and smaller warships, unseen by the RAF. That same day Luftwaffe reconnaissance discovered the first group of troopships, but this convoy – 240km south-east of Marschall's squadron and headed south-west – was thought to be empty hulls returning to the UK.

The next morning Marschall encountered the empty tanker *Oil Pioneer* steaming from Tromsø with only one armed trawler as an escort. Neither vessel had a chance to send a distress message and both were quickly sunk with only 29 survivors.

Shortly afterwards the *Scharnhorst*'s Ar 196 floatplane discovered the *Orama* and *Atlantis* to the north and the Flottenchef dispatched *Admiral Hipper* and the destroyers to intercept. The *Orama* tried to send an urgent SOS, but this was jammed by the *Admiral Hipper*'s radio operator and the *Atlantis*, obeying the rules of war, sent no signals else it forfeit its immunity from attack. The *Orama* succumbed to the *Admiral Hipper*'s 20.3cm guns and sank as the smaller warships drew up to rescue the 275 survivors. Afterwards this force steered for the shelter of Trondheimfjord.

The main batteries of the *Gneisenau* and *Scharnhorst* open fire on HMS *Glorious*. (Courtesy Imperial War Museum, London – HU3287)

Aboard HMS *Ark Royal* FAA Skua dive-bombers are prepared for the attack against the German battle squadron at Trondheim. Only seven would return. (FAA Museum)

Just as the Narvik evacuation went undetected by the Luftwaffe, the presence of Adm. Marschall's squadron was still unobserved by the British despite the fact the seas were alive with elements of the Home Fleet. Without interference by German surface ships or submarines for two months, complacency had settled heavily on RN commanders. For instance, the *Glorious* steamed homewards at a sedate 17 knots with only two thirds of her boilers operating and no aircraft armed and ready. Captain D'Oyly Hughes did not even post lookouts in the crow's nest, much less launch his Swordfish TSR biplanes to scout out ahead of his vulnerable carrier and its meagre escort. Thus it was a great surprise when, at 1600hrs that afternoon, the two German battlecruisers hove into view, steaming directly at the carrier at flank speed.

The two destroyers, *Ardent* and *Acasta*, made smoke but this did little to spoil the Germans' aim and the first salvo – launched at 25,600m with typical German accuracy – thundered out at 1630hrs. Within minutes hits blasted the hangar deck forward and the Hurricanes crowded there

burst into flames that spread rapidly from one aircraft to another. As the battlecruisers closed, jamming the *Glorious'* distress signals as they came, they pounded the hapless carrier repeatedly. Soon the ship was a blazing hulk dead in the water, listing heavily. Hurriedly abandoned, she capsized and sank at 1740hrs.

Meanwhile the two destroyers did what they could with smoke, gunfire and torpedo attacks. The *Ardent* attacked first, punching through the smokescreen to close and launch eight torpedoes. The battlecruisers' secondary batteries blasted it into a careering, blazing wreck that rolled over and sank at 1728hrs. At that time *Acasta*, too, turned back to attack and, in a gallant last gesture, put a torpedo into the side of the *Scharnhorst* just beneath the aft turret. This hit killed 48, knocked out two of the battlecruiser's engine rooms and reduced her speed to 20 knots. *Acasta* did not survive the attack. Riddled with heavy hits, ablaze over most of her length, she sank 40 minutes later.

Of the valiant RN crews and RAF aviators – a total of 1,559 men – only 40 survived, rescued by two passing Norwegian vessels and a patrolling German seaplane. Only two RAF pilots, Squadron Leader Kenneth B. B. Cross, commander of No. 46 Squadron, and Flight Lieutenant P. G. Jameson, were among them.

As Marschall headed his two capital ships to Trondheim, the second group of troopships, bearing nearly 10,000 troops, escorted by the AA cruiser *Coventry* (Vivian's flagship) and two destroyers departed Andfjord. They were joined by HMS *Ark Royal*, *Southampton* and three destroyers. Aboard the light cruiser were Lord Cork and Orrery, Maj. Gen. Auchinleck and Gén. de brig. Béthouart. From Tromsø the cruiser *Devonshire* sailed singly with King Håkon, his government and Gen.Maj. Fleischer aboard.

Incredibly, it was not until HMS *Valiant* met *Atlantis* the next day that the RN even realized Marschall's squadron had been at large in the area. That day Gen.Maj. Ruge disbanded his army and began negotiations to surrender his nation to the Germans.

FAA SKUA ATTACK ON THE *SCHARNHORST* IN TRONDHEIMFJORD, 13 JUNE 1940 (pages 86–87)

In an effort to extract some retribution for the loss of HMS *Glorious*, and to attempt a repeat of the FAA's brilliant dive-bombing victory over the *Königsberg* at Bergen two months prior, at 0100hrs on 13 June 1940 HMS *Ark Royal* launched 15 Blackburn Skua dive-bombers (1) to attack the Kriegsmarine's battle squadron while it rode peacefully at anchor at Trondheim Harbour following Operation *Juno*. Led by Lieutenant-Commander John Casson, the formation approached from the north at 0243hrs, in clear skies and broad daylight typical of the northerly latitude and time of year. Alerted by the premature arrival of RAF Beauforts attacking Værnes airfield, Messerschmitts were airborne and attacked the incoming raiders over the fjord, forcing a confusing series of defensive reactions. Approaching the target – the battlecruiser *Scharnhorst* (2) – Casson led No. 803 NAS in their diving attacks first and lost four aircraft, including his own, shot down. Captain R. T. Partridge followed with No. 800 NAS, diving into a maelstrom of flak from the ship below. His bomb missed, but his wingman, Lieutenant Kenneth V. V. Spurway followed suit and placed his 500lb SAP bomb (3) on the starboard side abaft the funnel. Unfortunately it failed to detonate. Captain Partridge was shot down during egress to become a POW for the rest of the war. Spurway and the second wingman, Petty Officer (Airman) H. A. Monk, escaped seawards, but the next three Skuas were all shot down, bringing the total to eight aircraft lost and no damaging hits achieved. For the Blackburn Skua, this was its last hurrah. Because of high attrition rates it was withdrawn from frontline service shortly afterwards.

While the land and sea battles in Norway were over, there was still one air operation to be played out before the campaign was fully concluded. With the two German battlecruisers lying at anchor in Trondheimfjord, the RN hoped to repeat its initial success against berthed warships by sending in its FAA Skua fighter/dive-bombers to inflict hopefully crippling damage.

On 13 June, the Home Fleet steamed within attack range of the sheltering fjord and HMS *Ark Royal* launched 15 Skuas, nine from No. 803 NAS led by Lieutenant-Commander. John Casson, RN, and six from No. 800 NAS, led by Captain Richard T. Partridge, RM, while another three (No. 800 NAS) flew a combat air patrol over the task force. This time, however, the two squadrons had none of the advantages they possessed two months before, except clear weather.

A pre-emptive airfield attack on the Luftwaffe fighters at Værnes by RAF Beaufort twin-engine fighter-bombers accomplished little other than alerting the Germans that something was up. In response Bf 109Es and Bf 110s scrambled to become airborne. Meanwhile the two FAA squadrons winged in over the large fjord, angling in from the north at an altitude of 3,050m, splitting up to conduct separate attacks. As they approached the AA fire from both the ships and shore batteries reached up to greet them, filling the air ahead with angry, ugly bursts.

Lieutenant-Commander Casson led most of his squadron around to one side to attack from stern to bow, while Capt. Partridge led No. 800 NAS set up to attack from the opposite direction. Ravaged by squadrons of Messerschmitts and met by horrific flak Lt. Cdr. Casson and three other No. 803 NAS Skuas were shot down in flames. From the other side Capt. Partridge and another three No. 800 NAS Skuas were hit and flamed, with Partridge bailing out to become a POW.

Only one bomb hit the *Scharnhorst* and it proved to be a dud. The seven survivors of the early morning strike landed aboard *Ark Royal* at 0345hrs and the task force headed back to Scapa Flow in fog so thick that two escorting destroyers collided and were badly damaged.

AFTERMATH

On 28 July the remains of the German battle fleet – one battle-cruiser, one heavy cruiser, a light cruiser and four destroyers – arrived back at Kiel. Essentially these were all that remained of the 22 modern Kriegsmarine warships (destroyers and larger) that set sail from German ports almost four months before. Grossadmiral Raeder was once quoted as saying that having Norway was worth the loss of half his fleet. The cost was almost exactly that for his audacious enterprise.

The true measure of any military campaign is whether it achieved its objectives. For the Germans, *Weserübung* successfully brought little Denmark and the long coastline of Norway into the Third Reich. German military efficiency in all arms, and superiority in all but the navy, resulted in the conquest of Norway in only 60 days despite the bravery of the Norwegian defence, the tireless efforts of the Royal Navy and the mobilization of the first Allied expeditionary force of World War II.

But was it truly worth it? The Kriegsmarine, which had stood to gain the most from the conquest, was crippled in doing so. The Germans lost one (of two) heavy cruisers, two (of six) light cruisers, ten (of 20) destroyers and six U-boats. In the epilogue to this campaign, on the initial attempt to return to Kiel on 20 June, the *Gneisenau* was torpedoed by the British submarine *Clyde*, which blew a hole through her bow and, like her sister ship *Scharnhorst*, put her in dry dock for the rest of the year. Consequently, the Kriegsmarine was down to a solitary heavy cruiser, two light cruisers and four destroyers operational, making the contemplated cross-Channel invasion of England in the autumn of 1940 out of the question.

Nevertheless, the Germans reaped some operational advantages, providing lairs for its few remaining capital ships – such as the mighty *Tirpitz*, then under construction – at Tromsø and Trondheim, as well as threatening the convoy route to the USSR during the dark days of 1942–43. But this was a sideshow compared to the Battle of the Atlantic and it was the capture of Brest as a result of the fall of France that provided the submarine pens to pursue the U-boat campaign against the convoys from Canada and the USA that sustained Great Britain as a nation and as a base for the Allies' return to Continental Europe in 1944.

However, more importantly, the single campaign resulted in the eventual demise of the German surface fleet. From the seeds sown in the crippling losses of *Weserübung*, the loss of the *Bismarck* in Operation *Rheinübung*, and finally the failure of the regroupment of Kriegsmarine surface ships in Norway – specifically the failure of the *Admiral Hipper*, *Lützow* and six destroyers against the Russia-bound convoy JW51B in December 1942 – completely destroyed Hitler's confidence in his navy's capabilities. Consequently, in January 1943 he ordered all major fleet units 'paid off' and their big guns mounted in the Atlantic Wall and other

King Håkon VII and Crown Prince Olaf during the Norwegian campaign. Without King Håkon's resolute determination to fight the Nazi invaders, this campaign, and all the lessons it taught the Allies, would have never occurred. (Courtesy Imperial War Museum, London – HU55637)

Vizeadmiral Günther Lütjens proved a formidable adversary, leading German capital ships on subsequent forays, but in May 1941 he went down with the *Bismarck*. (Courtesy Imperial War Museum, London – A14897)

Major-General Claude Auchinleck went on to command British forces against Rommel in North Africa and eventually became the C.-in-C. in India. (Courtesy Imperial War Museum, London – E4559)

coastal defences. He now placed his faith in unrestricted submarine warfare. With the shift to the undersea campaign, Grossadmiral Raeder was not needed. On 30 January he was succeed by Adm. Karl Dönitz, head of the Kriegsmarine U-boat arm.

On land the cost of holding their conquests proved more expensive than the acquisition. Most of von Falkenhorst's divisions remained in Norway to protect the precious prize. Denmark, favoured as the Nazi's 'model protectorate', did not take lightly to the heavy-handed occupation and, by August 1943, Danish resistance activities resulted in a tyrannical crackdown. By then the little nation was occupied by 170,000 German troops, keeping the equivalent of 14 divisions away from the fronts.

On the other side, the British showing in the first face-to-face combat with the Germans was a dismal disappointment. Surprised by the Nazi's first moves and almost casually handing the initiative to a ruthless enemy, hamstrung by slipshod operational planning and unworkable command arrangements, defeated in detail on the ground and absolutely incapable of countering the might or effectiveness of the Luftwaffe in the air, the British had a lot to learn about modern warfare.

The surface warship losses incurred by the Allied navies in the campaign – one heavy cruiser, one AA cruiser, ten destroyers and sloops, and five submarines – could be sustained. It was the shattering loss of the *Glorious* – one of only four RN carriers extant – and the painful lack of carrier-based fighters and the pitiful ineffectiveness of shipboard AA guns that proved to be the foremost lessons. These would take years – and much American *matériel* – to correct.

Generalmajor Otto Ruge was determined and dignified to the last and after five years' imprisonment, returned to Norway to once again command his nation's armed forces. (Norwegian Resistance Museum)

In the final analysis *Weserübung* was a costly enterprise that benefited the victor little. But as a joint campaign it set the standard and pattern for all other air-land-sea offensives that followed it, including the Allies' successful return to the European Continent in Operation *Overlord*. Thus, while *Weserübung* may have cost a lot and benefited Germany little, it taught valuable lessons to Hitler's adversaries, lessons that were eventually used to break the Nazi grip on Western Europe.

THE BATTLEFIELD TODAY

On the battlefields of Norway little evidence remains today of the tumultuous struggle that occurred there some 65 years ago. This is principally because of the growth of the cities at which these clashes occurred and the development of businesses and urban neighbourhoods across the battlefields. For example, the pivotal Fornebu Airport at Oslo was closed in 1998 and is now a business park.

Because of its isolation, Narvik provides the battlefields most unchanged by the expanse of human progress. For example, the Post Pier, the site of the initial landings of the *Gebirgsjäger*, still stands, minus one of its buildings destroyed by an errant British torpedo on 13 April. The most significant original structure in the town is the ore railway power station, which is little changed except for its new roof. Orneset Beach just to the east of town, where the French Foreign Legion and the Norwegian 15th Regiment came ashore to recapture Narvik, is largely unchanged. Farther to the east, at Sildvik on the south shore of Rombakfjord, the rusted prow of the only remaining German destroyer – the valiant *Georg Thiele* – can be viewed jutting from the water where it was run ashore ending the desperate battle of 13 April. Finally a Hotchkiss H-39 tank – among other artefacts from the conflict – can be viewed in Narvik at the Nordland Red Cross War Museum.

Most resilient to change has been the concrete bunkers and gun emplacements of the Norwegian coastal forts. For example, at Oscarsborg the embrasures and ancient 28cm guns that sank the *Blücher* can still be seen. However, the fortress remains in use as a training centre, so access is limited and must be coordinated in advance.

In addition, some of the most significant elements of the campaign have been preserved in museums, the most important of which is the Forsvarsmuseet (Armed Forces Museum) at the old Fort Akershus, the ancient bastion guarding Oslo's inner harbour that also served as the depot of the Norwegian 1st Division in 1940. Norwegian army and naval armaments from 1940, and even some German equipment such as an Enigma machine and an Hs 293 guided missile can be seen. The Forsvarsmuseet's aircraft collection is located at Gardermoen, the former depot of the 2nd Division and now Oslo's commercial airport.

Finally, in memorial to the 11,530 men who were killed in the course of the campaign, several small monuments are emplaced at significant locations. For instance, most significantly, at Narvik there are two stone markers on Orneset Beach signifying the spots where French and Norwegian troops came ashore to liberate the town briefly. Bringing us full circle, there is even a small memorial in Jøssingfjord marking the point where the *Altmark*'s stern touched the shore during the famous incident that sparked the entire operation called *Weserübung*.

FURTHER READING

Because no comprehensive history of the 1940 campaign in Norway and Denmark exists, further research must locate a number of publications to obtain the view from each of the many sides of this campaign.

The best source for understanding the German side of the campaign is actually Telford Taylor's *March of Conquest: German Victories in Western Europe, 1940* (New York: Simon and Schuster, 1958). While *Weserübung* forms only a portion of this larger work, Taylor relates the German decisions, planning, deployment and operations in finite detail at the diplomatic, strategic and operational levels. It is lacking however in detail of the tactical and small unit engagements.

The most comprehensive history of the Norwegian campaign from the British perspective is T. K. Derry's *The Campaign in Norway*, edited by J. R. M. Butler (first published by HMSO, 1952). As the government's official history it is quite naturally not unbiased and consequently downplays the contributions of the Norwegians to the defence of their own nation, demeans the French participation and overstates the damage done to the Germans. For detailed account of British ground actions Christopher Buckley's *Norway* (London: HMSO, 1951) is without peer for detailed descriptions of units, deployments, battles and results.

From the naval side, RN Captain Donald Macintyre's *Narvik* (New York: W. W. Norton & Company, Inc., 1960) tells the story principally from the Allied perspective in exciting and sublime detail, but suffers from its judgemental editorializing. For a completely even-handed and exceedingly detailed account of both battles in Ofotfjord, Captain Peter Dickens (also RN), *Narvik: Battles in the Fjords* (Annapolis, MD: Naval Institute Press, 1974) is highly recommended. It is the sort of history every author should strive to achieve.

The Norwegian campaign was largely won through the one side's almost total domination of its air power. This story is told, in precise detail as a chronology, by Christopher Shores and a bevy of supporting researchers and writers in *Fledgling Eagles* (London: Grub Street, 1991). Although this volume covers the entire period of the 'Phoney War', the 142 pages (of 354) covering the Norwegian campaign provide the only detailed account of air actions in the campaign.

There are no English-language references for the Norwegian military in the defence of its nation. However, two books by Norwegian authors – Johan Waake's *The Narvik Campaign* (London: George G. Harrap & Co. Ltd, 1964) and Theodor Broch's *The Mountains Can Wait* (St Paul, WI: Webb Book Publishing Company, 1942) – include some information on Norwegian units in their somewhat stylized accounts of operations at Narvik.

For an English-language account of the French participation in Norway Captain Pierre Lapie's *With the Foreign Legion at Narvik* (London: John Murray, 1941) is recommended. There are two excellent books on the participation of the Polish Brigade: *The Fight for Narvik: Impressions of the Polish Campaign in Norway* by Karol Zbyszewski and Jozef Natanson (London: Lindsay Drummond, 1940) and *Polish Troops in Norway: A Photographic Record of the Campaign at Narvik* (London: M. I. Kolin, 1943).

Whatever their limitations or bias, all of the above should be studied together as a corporate body of work for the best understanding of this very complex campaign.

Bibliography

Ailsby, Christopher, *Hitler's Sky Warriors: German Paratroopers in Action 1939–1945*, Dulles, VA: Brassey's Inc., 2000

'Attack on Vaerlose Airfield', Peter Nellemann (trans.), originally printed in Danish in NYT, the magazine of IPMS Denmark, reprinted in *Small Air Forces Observer*, Vol. 14/2 (54), April 1990

Barnett, Correlli, *Engage the Enemy More Closely*, New York: W. W. Norton & Company, 1991

Boatner, Mark M., III, *The Biographical Dictionary of World War II*, Novato, CA: Presidio Press, 1996

Brayley, Martin, *Men-at-Arms 354: The British Army 1939–45 (1) North-West Europe*, Oxford: Osprey Publishing Ltd, 2001

Broch, Theodor, *The Mountains Wait* St. Paul, WI: Webb Book Publishing Company, 1942

Brown, Eric, 'Blackburn's ill-fated duo: The Skua and Roc', *Air International*, Vol. 13/4, November 1977

Buckley, Christopher, *Norway*, London: HMSO, 1951

Chesneau, Roger, *Aircraft Carriers of the World, 1914 to the Present*, London: Brockhampton Press, 1998

Crawford, Alex, *Gloster Gladiator*, Redbourne: Mushroom Models Publications, 2002

Derry, T. K., *The Campaign in Norway*, HMSO, 1952

Dickens, Peter, *Narvik: Battles in the Fjords*, Annapolis, MD: Naval Institute Press, 1974

Folsom, Russ, 'Panzers in Norway – 1940,' as published on website
http://hem.fyristorg.com/robertm/norge/Panzer%20Abt.%20z.b.V.40.html

Foss, Christopher (ed.), *Encyclopedia of Tanks and Armored Fighting Vehicles*, San Diego, CA: Thunder Bay Press, 2002

Frischauer, Willi, and Jackson, Robert, *The Altmark Affair*, New York: The Macmillan Company, 1955

Green, William, 'Stopper in the Bottle', *Air International*, Vol 17/4, October 1979

Hagen, Kurt Erik, 'Aldi Mer 9.April', *Small Air Forces Observer*, Vol 14/3 (55), July 1990

Hogg, Ian V., *Fortress: A History of Military Defense*, New York: St. Martin's Press Inc., 1977

Hooten, E. R., *Phoenix Triumphant: The Rise and Rise of the Luftwaffe*, London: Arms and Armour Press, 1994

Kersaudy, Francois, *Norway 1940*, New York: St. Martin's Press Inc., 1990

Konstam, Angus, *New Vanguard 88: British Battlecruisers 1939–45*, Oxford: Osprey Publishing Ltd, 2003

Lapie, Pierre O., *With the Foreign Legion at Narvik*, London: John Murray Ltd, 1941

Lenton, H. T., *German Warships of the Second World War*, New York: Arco Publishing Company Inc., 1976

Lucas, James, *Alpine Elite: German Mountain Troops of World War II*, London: Jane's Publishing Company Ltd, 1980

Lucas, James, *Storming Eagles: German Airborne Forces in World War Two*, London: Arms and Armour Press, 1988

Macintyre, Donald, *Narvik*, New York: W. W. Norton & Company Inc., 1960

Mallmann Showell, Jak P., *German Navy in World War Two*, Annapolis, MD: Naval Institute Press, 1979

Mollo, Andrew, *Armed Forces of World War II Uniforms, Insignia and Organization*, London: Orbis Publishing, 1981

Morzik, General Fritz, *German Air Force Airlift Operations*, New York: Arno Press, 1968

Pallud, Jean Paul, *After the Battle: The Norwegian Campaign*, London: After the Battle, 2004

Quarrie, Bruce, *Battle Orders 4: German Airborne Divisions: Blitzkrieg 1940–41*, Oxford: Osprey Publishing Ltd, 2004

Quarrie, Bruce, *Men-at-Arms 139: German Airborne Troops 1939–45*, Oxford: Osprey Publishing Ltd, 1983.

Roskill, S. W., *White Ensign: The British Navy at War 1939–1945*, Annapolis, MD: Naval Institute Press, 1960

Shores, Christopher, Foreman, John, Ehrengardt, Christian-Jacques, Weiss, Heinrich, and Olson, Bjorn, *Fledgling Eagles: The Complete Account of Air Operations During the 'Phoney War' and Norwegian Campaign, 1940*, London: Grub Street, 1991

Smith, Peter C., *Into the Assault: Famous Dive Bomber Aces of the Second World War*, London: John Murray Ltd, 1985

Sumner, Ian, and Vauvillier, Francois, *Men-at-Arms 315: The French Army 1939–45 (Vol 1)*, Oxford: Osprey Publishing Ltd, 2000

Tarnstrom, Ronald L., *Germany: The Wehrmacht Strikes: 1940–1942*, Lindsborg, KA: Trogen Books, 1989

Tarnstrom, Ronald L., *Sword of Scandinavia*, Lindsborg, KA: Trogen Books, 1982

Taylor, Telford, *March of Conquest: German Victories in Western Europe, 1940*, New York: Simon and Schuster, 1958

Thomas, Andrew, *Aircraft of the Aces 44: Gloster Gladiator Aces*, Oxford: Osprey Publishing, 2002

Waage, Johan, *The Narvik Campaign*, London: George G. Harrap & Co. Ltd, 1964

Weal, John, *Aircraft of the Aces 25: Messerschmitt Bf 110 Zerströrer Aces of World War 2*, Oxford: Osprey Publishing, 1999

Whitley, M. J., *Battleships of World War Two*, London: Arms and Armour, 1998

Whitley, M. J., *Cruisers of World War Two*, London: Brockhampton Press, 1999

Williamson, Gordon, *New Vanguard 71: German Battleships 1939–45*, Oxford: Osprey Publishing Ltd, 2003

Williamson, Gordon, *New Vanguard 91: German Destroyers 1939–45*, Oxford: Osprey Publishing Ltd, 2003

Williamson, Gordon, *New Vanguard 81: German Heavy Cruisers 1939–45*, Oxford: Osprey Publishing Ltd, 2003

Williamson, Gordon, *New Vanguard 84: German Light Cruisers 1939–45*, Oxford: Osprey Publishing Ltd, 2003

Williamson, Gordon, *New Vanguard 75: German Pocket Battleships 1939–45*, Oxford: Osprey Publishing Ltd, 2003

Williamson, Gordon, *Elite 63: German Mountain & Ski Troops 1939–45*, Oxford: Osprey Publishing Ltd, 1996

Zaloga, Steven J., *Men-at-Arms 117: The Polish Army 1939–45*, Oxford: Osprey Publishing Ltd, 1982

INDEX

References to illustrations are shown in **bold**.